HOW TO TELL A GREAT STORY (2ND EDITION)

A book for the novice storyteller looking to learn the basics of storytelling in a weekend.

Aneeta Sundararaj

Copyright © 2020 Aneeta Sundararaj

All rights reserved

The characters and events portrayed in this book are fictitious. Any similarity to real persons, living or dead, is coincidental and not intended by the author.

No part of this book may be reproduced, or stored in a retrieval system, or transmitted in any form or by any means, electronic, mechanical, photocopying, recording, or otherwise, without express written permission of the publisher.

ISBN-13: 9798557295291

For the columnists, both past and present, of my online newsletter, Great StoryTelling Network.

CONTENTS

Title Page	1
Copyright	2
Dedication	3
Introduction	7
Ammachi	11
Step 1 - Vital Preparation	17
Step 2 - Themes of Your Great Story	31
Step 3 – The Reasons for Telling Your Great Story	42
Step 4 - It's All About the People	55
Step 5 – Paint Your Setting	66
Step 6 - Join The Dots	76
Step 7 – It's All a Matter of Style	85
Conclusion	102
Appendix A – Planning and Analysing Your Research Material	104
Appendix B – Information for market research	106
Appendix C: Character Profile	107
Appendix D – Sample Storyline	110
Appendix E – Copyright Issues for Storytellers	112
Bibliography	117
What Others Are Saying About 'How To Tell A Great Story'	119

About the Author 121
About How To Tell A Great Story 123

INTRODUCTION

Stories are indispensable to human culture.
Okey Ndibe

What is storytelling? From the many people I've interviewed over the years, I've come to realise that there are many answers to this question. For instance, where Linda Gorham says "Storytelling is an oral art," David Bowman says "[a] good story is a good story regardless of the medium."

Perhaps, the most comprehensive answer to this question is the one given by Hayley Hunkin, who says "Stories are the basis of human communication. We have been telling stories before we could write throughout human history… It is important to share out stories, whether it is in a more 'journalistic' format of writing articles, or writing creative short stories and novels."

I would add to this by saying that a story doesn't have to appear in words alone. A photograph can tell a story. Take the one below which I took in Cambodia. Sometimes, when I look at it, I think that the man is greeting the morning sun, as though he's saying, "Hello Sun." Look closely and you'll see that he's actually extending his fishing net high above his head, preparing for the day's haul.

What of the storyteller, then? Although Ruth Kirkpatrick says "Stories are all around us and we are all storytellers," I have envisaged this book for people who are completely new to storytelling; who have no clue where to begin, what to do and how to go about getting ideas for their stories. This book is not for people who have already started to tell their stories or even sell them. **This book is for the novice storyteller.**

Since you have the complete book in your hands, you can flick through it in any order. However, you will get the most benefit from this book if you go through the steps in the order that they are set out as each one builds on the one before it. As you learn a step, try it out. Then, move on to the next step until you come up with a complete story. If you would like to, adopt Jim Cyr's words and view this book as "an experienced storyteller who can mentor you with encouragement and wisdom."

I think the key to being a good storyteller is to listen, to listen with a clean slate, to the voice of the people and to their silences, to the streets, to the forests even to the sky.

Valentina Ortiz

Where appropriate, I've inserted advice given by many of the storytellers I've interviewed (such as the one above) for my website (http://www.howtotellagreatstory.com) under the column called *Blow Your Own Trumpet!* The main aim of this column is to allow the person I interview to market their products/books/services to my readers. In all the interviews that I work on, I try to make it a point to ask one question which will be of most benefit to my readers: *What advice would these storytellers give others who would like to become storytellers?* Some of the answers given by these storytellers are long, some are short and some make me laugh. My hope is that each time you feel despondent, alone, dejected or in need of some comfort, the words of these storytellers will inspire you to carry on telling your story.

In addition, this book has a "creative writing" slant to the text. This is because I am involved in creative writing projects and my storytelling is influenced by what I learn there. Nevertheless, my experience shows that storytelling does play a vital role in business and non-fiction work as well. Therefore, the way I see it, the creative writing element can only enhance what I share. As Noël Gama says, "storytelling is not only about fiction – it takes non-fiction from being merely factual to being real."

The English used in this book is "UK English" – which means that the spelling for words used follows those used in the UK rather than in any other English-speaking country. For example, where in America one would spell it as "color", in the UK (and also in this book), the word is spelt as "colour".

Finally, before we proceed to Step 1, let me share a story with you. I am aware that most authors will share a story as a bonus and publish towards the end of the book. I wanted to do something special. Treat the story below as a taste of the adventure you're about to embark on. It was first published on my website, then included in the collection of short stories mentioned above, *Two Snakes Whistling at the Same Time*. The story is called *Ammachi*, and remains one of my most popular ones ever.

AMMACHI

I grew up sharing my birthday with an unforgettable woman, Godavari Pillay. To me, she was simply "Ammachi", which is Malayalam for "grandmother". We're not related by blood or marriage, but I've known her since forever. By the time I was born, Ammachi was already a widow. She and her late husband, Dr Pillay, had made their home in Butterworth.

My memories of that house in Butterworth are vivid. Built on a corner lot facing the beach, there was a wide balcony that went all the way round the first floor. Many nights, while the adults turned over sausages and meat patties sizzling away on a coal-fired barbecue, we little ones leaned against the cement balcony and gazed at the flickering lights of tall buildings miles away on Penang Island.

If you "popped in" to visit Ammachi, be prepared to be greeted by a furious lady. Standing at the threshold of her home, she'd scowl and say, "How can you come here and not tell me beforehand?" Her hospitality challenged, she'd say she hadn't had time to prepare your favourite dish. This was in spite of having at least seven dishes already laid out on her long dining table.

Truth be told, Ammachi overwhelmed many with her love and affection. She didn't merely visit the ill; she stayed with them and nursed them back to health for as long as she could. If you happened to mention that you liked cream cheese, on her next visit, she would bring along bottles of them in every shape, size and variety. And if your child was of marriageable age, whisper to Ammachi that you were looking for a suitable match for this child. She may force you to move cities and towns, but, by hook or by crook, a marriage would be arranged in no time at all.

It's precisely what happened with my parents. I imagine that both my grandmothers had a few quiet and worry-filled words with Ammachi. After all, in the 1960s, my parents were already in their mid-thirties and still single. Ammachi set her mind to getting my parents married and, in less than three months, Godavari Pillay made the Cinnasami family happen. On 2 April 2016, my parents celebrated their fiftieth wedding anniversary.

This was all very well and good, but none of it mattered on my fourth birthday. Standing on a stool, on one side of our dining table, I frowned deeply. I heard my classmate from the Methodist Kindergarten say to another one of our friends, "She so lucky, one. Her cake so nice."

Yes, I should have felt lucky. I should be smiling from ear to ear. I should be showing off this wonderful cake. But it was impossible to muster the tiniest of smiles. My dream was turning into a nightmare. Maybe, Mummy would understand my dilemma.

"No, Tara. Ammachi is like your third grandmother," Mummy said, failing miserably to pacify me. "You must be the superstar here and share with her."

Share the cake?

Share?

This was my cake.

Not our cake.

My cake.

Certainly, by virtue of Ammachi's position as my third grandmother, I am proud that I am sometimes Tara Chechi to some of my younger "siblings", a younger sister to others and a niece to several uncles and aunts, even though I don't have an ounce of Malayalee blood. But I wasn't going to share this cake with her if I had a choice in the matter.

This birthday cake was special. There was a cottage with white birds perched on the roof. In the garden, there was a little English girl with blond hair (obviously me in a previous incarnation) playing with my pet rabbit. During the planning stages which lasted two months, I refused to settle for a two-dimensional creation with royal icing rosettes and a shaky "Happy Birthday Tara" written by someone who was probably suffering from the early onset of Parkinson's. Mine was going to be a three-dimensional baking wonder, something unique that Alor Setar folk of 1976 had never seen before.

It was a special cake made especially for me.

Not me and Ammachi.

It was too much, this having to "share-share".

Just too much.

All this angst as a child means that, today, I go into a mild panic when people tell me that their birthdays (or children's birthdays) are in November. I am relieved when they confirm that it's not the fourth as I don't think I would like a child to feel that same frustration I felt at having to share a birthday with another person.

My fourth birthday was also the start of the tension-filled relationship the child Tara had with Ammachi. And Ammachi did little to help ease the said tension. How she made me wake up to stand facing the rising sun and recite the *Gayathri* mantra with her. This was a good thing, of course. But at 6.30 in the morning? I was grumpy, sleepy, hungry and all of five years old.

There was a time when my penitent prayer was that Ammachi would stop going to visit her daughter in Australia. That way, I wouldn't have to hear, repeatedly, about her talented grandson, Moni.

"You know, Moni can play 'Maiden's Prayer' so well," Ammachi would tell Mummy. "And, today, I timed Tara. She only practised for nine minutes. She won't play like Moni if she doesn't practise."

No one cared that I didn't like playing the piano. I still don't. I don't mind listening to others play, but I would rather crochet, paint, carve wood, do cross-stitch ... anything, except play the piano. Still, I was damned if Moni was going to do better than me. I forced my seven-year-old fingers to practise playing "Maiden's Prayer". I didn't know half of what the symbols on the music score meant and my fingers were so short that they could not even span an octave. So, I improvised and massacred the piece by making a staccato sound whenever there was an octave in the "Maiden's Prayer".

Two years ago, I visited Moni on his sprawling property on the outskirts of Brisbane. While an iguana lounged on the side of his pool and a possum gnawed at a mango, we sipped lemonade on the patio. We got to talking about Ammachi and, naturally, I told him this story about my determination to practise "Maiden's Prayer". He stared at me, incredulous, then threw his head back and laughed. He wiped away his tears and revealed a little secret. While I believed that he was this ever-so-diligent piano player, he believed the same of me. Apparently, Ammachi would tell something him along the lines of, "You know, Tara, she's only seven, but she can play the 'Maiden's Prayer' so well. If you don't practise, you'll never play the piano as well as her." Duly challenged, he, too, pushed himself to excel.

"That cheeky little devil," I replied, but with a big smile. She was crafty, this third grandmother of mine. Without an iota of malice, she'd played both her grandchildren against each other to ensure our success. And I loved her even more for it.

On 3 November 1984, something extraordinary happened. A week before, Ammachi had gone to see a doctor. It was decided that on 4 November 1984, Ammachi would have to undergo an operation to remove a cancerous growth. It's been so long now, that I had forgotten what kind of cancer it was.

The operation was to be carried out in Alor Setar General Hospital and she had a room in the first-class ward. Our house became base camp for her children and relatives to stay and commute to the hospital.

In the evening, I went with my parents to visit Ammachi. When we arrived, there was only a half-hour left until visiting hours were over. Daddy wasn't too perturbed. After all, he once worked in this hospital. Besides, his ex-boss was there too, among the twenty-odd visitors.

By 7.30 p.m., however, the crowd swelled to almost a hundred. Everyone from the who's who of the medical fraternity in Alor Setar was there—from medical superintendents, chief medical officers and their deputies to private practitioners. In addition to this lot were family members and way too many friends. This included one of Ammachi's newest neighbours, a couple she introduced to each other and their exotic beauty of a baby girl, Kamakshi.

The patient was, of course, in her element—Ammachi smiled, greeted them all, caught up with the latest gossip, arranged a few meetings between prospective brides and grooms and doled out advice to anyone who cared to listen. If she could command the kitchen staff to prepare meals for us all, she would have.

At 8 p.m., a young full-bearded doctor turned up. I will never forget what happened next. He stood at one end of the corridor, arms akimbo. He looked at all of Ammachi's visitors, took a deep breath and shouted, "G-E-T O-U-T!" He curled his lips before saying, "Everybody get out! The patient has a procedure tomorrow."

The more courageous ones filed past the doctor. Keeping close to the wall, they watched their every step. The cowards—the medical superintendents, chief medical officers, their deputies who had once worked in this hospital, my parents and I—used the back stairs to leave Alor Setar General Hospital. Daddy described what we did that day as "slinking away".

Ammachi's operation was successful. Sadly, she was only in remission for no more than a few years. By today's standards, Ammachi died too young as she was only 65 years old. I often wonder what else she could have achieved had she lived longer. Perhaps, she could have prevented a few more girls from becoming spinsters by getting them married off to suitable men; she would have taught a few more children the *Gayathri* mantra; or she could have seen her grandchildren become successful and responsible adults.

Since that fateful day in Alor Setar General Hospital, I have visited many an ill person. Not one, however, has come close to having the same number of visitors as Ammachi had in 1984. I live my life knowing that it is an honour to have witnessed this amazing occasion when almost a hundred people came to visit my third grandmother in the hospital on the eve of our birthday.

Now that you've enjoyed reading *Ammachi,* let's proceed to the first step in this storytelling adventure and get you firmly on the path of telling your own stories.

STEP 1 - VITAL PREPARATION

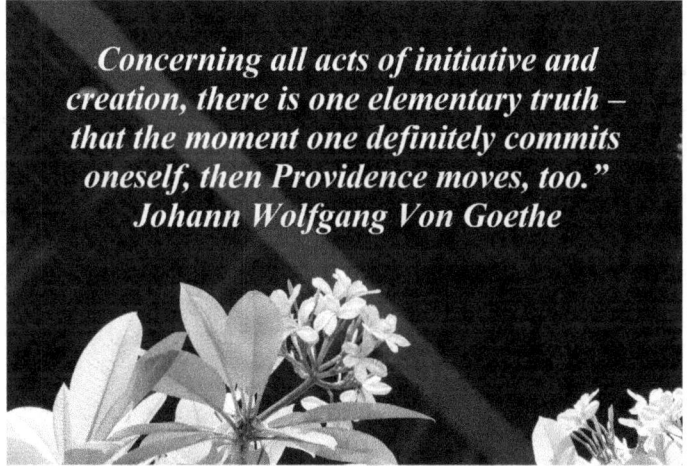

Concerning all acts of initiative and creation, there is one elementary truth – that the moment one definitely commits oneself, then Providence moves, too."
Johann Wolfgang Von Goethe

Imagine this: you are standing in an empty room. You are an artist and would like to paint a picture, but you have no canvas, no paints or brushes. There isn't even an easel. How are you possibly going to create your masterpiece without these basic items in hand? Likewise, in storytelling, if you do not have some of the most basic equipment in hand, how are you possibly going to tell that great story of yours?

The art of storytelling is not just about standing before a whole lot of people and saying the first thing that pops into your head. It is about communicating your thoughts, ideas and vision to people in an effective manner. It is about sharing your opinion with someone else. It is about recording your own history for future generations. Linda Garbe explains as follows:

I do an exercise in my seminars where a person speaks for five minutes about someone who has been very important in their life. I then ask the listeners to write down what they can conclude about the speaker. I am not asking about the person the speaker talked about; I am asking about the person who was speaking. It is amazing how much people can conclude from listening for only five minutes to someone they have never met. People are able to make statements about what the speaker values and what they would be like to work with. When I share the assessments with the speaker's co-workers or family, they attest to how on target the assessments are. ... People rarely understand they tell people who they are every time they talk.

Once you understand that you will reveal yourself when you tell a story, the next thing to accept is Denise Bertrand's advice that, "[t]here is a mental discipline needed to develop to tell a good story. One has to have time and commitment to shaping a story."

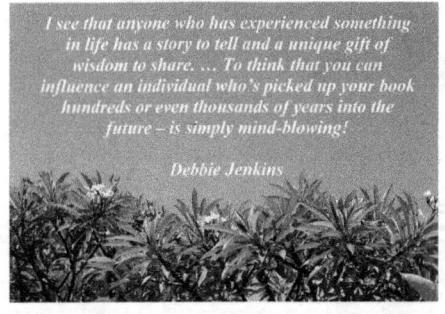

I see that anyone who has experienced something in life has a story to tell and a unique gift of wisdom to share. ... To think that you can influence an individual who's picked up your book hundreds or even thousands of years into the future – is simply mind-blowing!

Debbie Jenkins

Sometimes, storytellers who start out are fearful, shy or overwhelmed by the experience. There are any number of reasons for this – maybe, they have never set foot in a reference library or archives; maybe, they have never used the internet; maybe, the person they choose to interview is a stranger. If you experience any of these emotions, let me assure you that what you feel is completely normal. And, let me add that you don't need to feel this way at all. As Dennis Burnier Smith says, "Give it a go. Nothing is born from nothing; if you think you have a story to relate, put pen to paper, fingertips to keyboard and give substance to your thoughts. You never know, you could be the next JK Rowling." One of the best ways to deal with all these emotions is to carry out effective research.

Effective Research

Whatever kind story you tell, be it an article, play, short story, presentation, novel or even a photograph, sooner or later you will need to do some research. Research can encompass many things and it may involve any of the following:

- Checking a date, quotation or spelling.
- The name of a place you visited.
- The meaning of a specific phrase.
- The weather patterns in Eastern Europe in winter.

As Celise Downs says, "Do your homework because the research never stops." There is no magic formula or even special qualification to conduct effective research. You just simply build up knowledge of basic sources as you go along in an orderly fashion. I will suggest a few guidelines to help you. However, if you have developed your own way, by all means use it. If you'd like to share what you've learnt, I'd love to hear from you – just send an email to editor@howtotellagreatstory.com

The premise upon which you start your research should be this: it should bring you genuine happiness and a lasting enjoyment. It will, no doubt, add to your credibility and if you're lucky, expand your business network, if you have one.

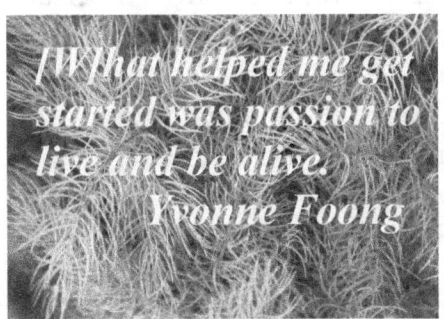
[W]hat helped me get started was passion to live and be alive.
— Yvonne Foong

Right Mental Attitude

Now that you've started to think about telling your own great story, it might be wise to warn you about the effort you'll need to put in. John di Lemme warns that, "As much as you may think your story is no big deal, your story will save someone's life ... Your story is powerful." There is, therefore, only one thing that separates a great storyteller and one who falls by the wayside and that's having the right mental attitude.

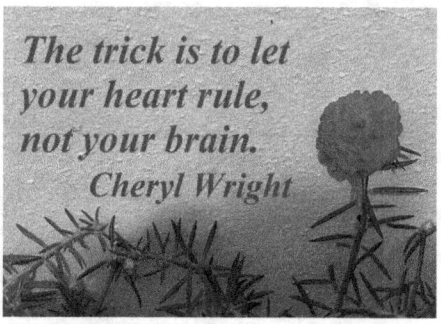

It's really easy to start with loads of enthusiasm, but very quickly run out of steam. If a storyteller is telling his story out loud and, if the story has no "oomph" factor, by the time he reaches the half-way point someone in the audience is sure to be yawning. As Michael LaRocca points out, "A bored storyteller is a boring storyteller."

You'll need to be firm with yourself and make a promise that you'll keep working at your stories, even if they no longer appeal to you with the same level of enthusiasm that they did in the beginning. You just need loads of determination and perseverance. With this kind of dedication to your storytelling, there's no stopping you.

Equipment

I do not know of anyone who would take up a new sport or leisure activity without the proper equipment. Likewise, if you choose to become a good storyteller you should not embark on your research unless you have the essential tools of the trade. The meaning of "essential" is subjective. There are some storytellers who just can't do without their tape recorders. There are those who are lost if they do not have notebooks. How much money you wish to spend on getting the right equipment is entirely up to you. In this piece I will provide you with a comprehensive, but in no way exhaustive, list of things I think you will need and what most storytellers use.

Writing Material
* Pens and pencils – if you're working with archived materials or

> ... [A]s far as the actual publishing is concerned, today everything in the publishing world has changed in just a few years due to computer capabilities.
>
> Steve Robertson

manuscript material in a library you will not be permitted to take notes other than by using a pencil.

* Paper – buy multi-purpose paper; the ones that can be used for photocopiers, faxes and ink-jet printers as well. If not, you'll find yourself buying three different kinds of paper and this can become extremely expensive.
* Notebooks – this depends entirely on what you're comfortable with – lined or ruled. I tend to use the ones where I can tear off and file later.
* A pocket stapler – this is far more useful than pins and clips.
* A ruler.
* A small magnifying glass.
* Highlighter.
* Clipboard.
* A desk lamp.
* A filing cabinet.
* A shelf to keep some basic reference books.

Personal Computers

> Use your library or the Internet to find stories.
> Susi Wolf

It is possible to write your stories by hand. However, in today's world, the reality is that anyone you would like to share your story with is likely to demand that the story be printed for them or emailed to them. If you are not computer savvy, it might be an idea to complete, at the very least, a basic course in how to use a computer. For those who are already computer savvy, you'll understand when I say that, as a storyteller, basic word-processing software is the feature in the computer that you're most likely to use. Indeed, Michelle Howe predicts that, "Storytelling on the Internet is even more viable today because of the use of audio and video on websites. The human voice is much more powerful than the written word."

Chris King, who has a website catering for storytellers says, "The biggest benefit to having an online presence is credibility. It has become expected of us. Even if a storyteller feels they don't want a full site of their own, they should be listed in as many storytelling directories as possible. They should, at least, consider setting up a blog (can be done, free of charge, at http://www.blogger.com). Having an online presence also keeps you informed as to what is happening in the storytelling community and makes the storyteller easy to contact by others who are searching."

Printers

I cannot emphasise enough the value of having a printer with you. This is because before you submit a story to anyone at all, you must print out one copy of the story. If not as a back up copy, at the very least, you'll note mistakes on paper easier than you will on the screen.

You are mistaken if you think that the spell-checker is good enough. For example, take the following sentence:

> The son rises in the esat.

The spell-checker will only note the error in the word "esat" not in the word "son", because "son" is a correct spelling, albeit the wrong word in terms of the meaning.

So, do invest in, or at least have access to, a printer.

Telephone and others

If you're not careful, when you start off in your storytelling adventure, you might find that you can end up with any number of the following machines:

* Telephone
* Fax machine
* Answering machine
* Photocopier
* Scanner
* Mobile phone
* External portable storage such as a Zip Drive, CD and/or DVD burner, and a thumb drive.

There is a way in which you can combine the features of some of the machines above and even do away with one or two. Indeed, you can have two of the same thing and not pay one cent more. This is how:

i. Invest in a telephone that also has fax and photocopying functions. [Note: sometimes a computer comes with inbuilt software that enables you to fax a document directly from your computer – this means you don't even have to print out the document before faxing it.]
ii. Invest in a printer that doubles up as a scanner and photocopier as well. See, you've got two photocopiers already!
iii. If you have a mobile phone, you might also have a free answering message service. Ask your land line phone company to divert all of the calls on your land to this mobile phone number and you will, therefore, have your messages stored on your mobile phone.

Camera

Some storytellers use photographs to enhance their stories. If you have a digital camera, this would be a wonderful way to enhance your stories. However, if you use the traditional camera, don't worry, the scanner from your printer would suffice. Also, there are many businesses that specialise in converting traditional photographs into digital form.

Reference Books

You can build up a reference library of your own over time. There is no necessity for you to rush out and buy only new copies of reference books. The following are just a handful of reference books I suggest. If you have an area of storytelling that you feel is better than any other, for example, storytelling for children, you should consider investing in reference books in your special area of storytelling.

1. The latest edition of *Writers and Artists' Yearbook*.
2. *The Concise Oxford Dictionary*
3. *Merriam-Webster's Collegiate Dictionary*
4. *Atlas of the World: Deluxe Edition*
5. *The Oxford Dictionary of Quotations*
6. *The Complete Plain Words* by Sir Ernest Gowers
7. *Usage and Abusage: A Guide to Good English*

Planning and Analysing Your Research

1. The first step is to plan your research. Do not hurry. Take a day or two and you will see the benefit of planning properly.

2. Do some brainstorming and, on an empty sheet of paper, make a summary of what you already know and a list of the main topics you think you will need to research a little more.

3. Begin with the internet. Start your research by logging on to the world wide web. If you can't do this from your own personal computer, you can go to a library, bookshop or any place that offers internet services.

4. The amount of information online is enormous. There are several search engines you can use. For instance:
   - http://www.google.com
   - http://www.msn.com
   - http://www.netscape.com
   - http://www.yahoo.com

5. The easiest way to explain how to compile the information

you gather through your research is to provide you with an example. For instance, you've found an article online called, "10 Laws of Storytelling'.

Note the following information down.
a) Date of Research: 15 March 2006
b) Title of resource: 10 Laws of Storytelling
c) Type of resource: Article
d) Media: electronic publication
e) Website URL: http://www.howtotellagreatstory.com/articles/article1.html
f) Author: Aneeta Sundararaj
g) Number of words: approximately 850
h) Excerpts:
> Law #1: Keep your mouth shut and your ears open.
> This is crucial in the first few moments of storytelling. Before you begin your story, take a moment. Look at your audience and smile at them. Only after you have got their attention do you begin to even introduce yourself and your topic. You will be able to observe many things about your audience in these few moments.

i) What was it about this story that made you want to read it?
   i. Did you want to know how to perform a specific task?
   ii. Was the subject matter of this story interesting/fascinating?
   iii. Was it informative?
   iv. Was it written in an entertaining manner? Can you give an exact example of what made it so?
   v. Was there a logical order to how the story was set out?
   vi. How did the story end?
   vii. Did you enjoy reading this story?
   viii. Would you read more work by this author?

j)   Copyright: Permitted to copy as long as due credit is given to author – see resource box.
k)   How to contact author:
     Email: editor@howtotellagreatstory.com
     Postal address: not available

To assist you, in Appendix A, I've prepared a template with this information for you. You are at liberty to print out this template as many times as you like to store your research.

6. One of the exciting things about this entire process is the fact that there can be spin-offs from the main research you do. You might well find new angles to your story or, in some cases, something that gives rise to a new story altogether.

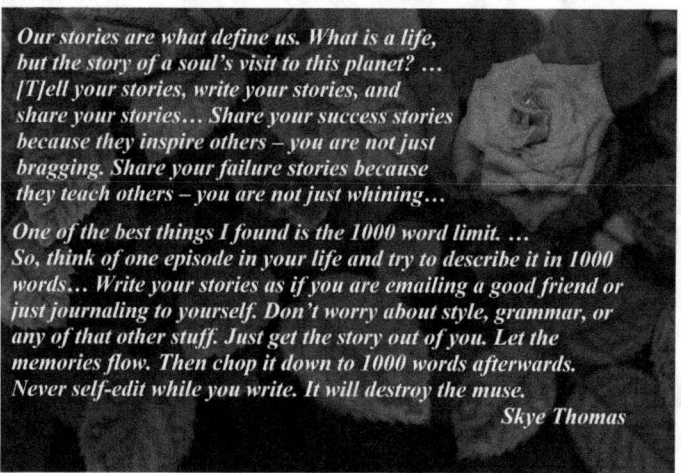

Our stories are what define us. What is a life, but the story of a soul's visit to this planet? ... [T]ell your stories, write your stories, and share your stories... Share your success stories because they inspire others – you are not just bragging. Share your failure stories because they teach others – you are not just whining...

One of the best things I found is the 1000 word limit. ... So, think of one episode in your life and try to describe it in 1000 words... Write your stories as if you are emailing a good friend or just journaling to yourself. Don't worry about style, grammar, or any of that other stuff. Just get the story out of you. Let the memories flow. Then chop it down to 1000 words afterwards. Never self-edit while you write. It will destroy the muse.

                                                            Skye Thomas

Storing Your Research Properly

Begin cataloguing every bit of research right from the very beginning. If you don't have the money to invest in a filing cabinet, a simple stack of boxes will do. There is no point in gathering a whole pile of notes and other material when, two months down the road, you have no clue what's in the pile. You might spend half a day looking for material, by which time you'd have disrupted not only your train of thought, but the flow of your story as well.

When your intention is to tell a story so that it sells, you need to know how to organise your market research so that you never fail when you submit work to a potential editor.

The first step is to know the kind of stories being told. What's popular these days? You need to understand the market you're targeting.

For works of fiction, one of the biggest mistakes you can make is to assume that bookshops are filled with the same sorts of stories that were sold ten years ago, or even five years ago. Pay particular interest to the trends in storytelling. Read as many novels as you can. Study the techniques used by successful novelists. Note how they use dialogue, characterisation and mood.

If you intend to tell your story orally, then listen to the stories that others tell. Get a feel of what entertains people today. Learn what's in fashion.

Whatever the manner in which you choose to tell your story, the requirements for market research remain the same. The following is a guideline you should use to help you organise your market research. For example, assume you'd like to write a short story for a magazine you're targeting. Here's what you need to take note of:

- Who is their target audience?
- What types of settings are suitable?
- What is the age range and gender of the people who generally read this magazine?
- Are the storylines in the magazines similar in all their stories?
- Is there any subject that is taboo – for instance, violence in any form or manner is unacceptable.
- How do you submit material to them? ie, do they accept submissions via email or do you have to send your submission by post?

To assist you, in Appendix B I've prepared a template with this information for you. You are at liberty to print out this template as many times as you like to store your research.

When you start to store the information you gather, begin big and break everything down into smaller and smaller categories.

For example, say you are interested in doing research about how a middle-class family lives.

Start with these words: FAMILY HOUSE MIDDLE-CLASS

Now, from FAMILY, divide it into Husband, Wife, Boys, Girls.

From HOUSE, divide it into Address, Big House, Small House, Number of Rooms, Cars, Bicycles, Motorbikes, Kitchen.

From MIDDLE CLASS, divide it into Income, Expenditure, Luxuries, Necessities.

Can you see the millions of permutations to this kind of organisation?

A word of advice, keep your "Big" files in alphabetical order.

Indeed, you may well find that you are constantly rearranging your "filing cabinet" as the volume of information you gather increases.

With the advent of computers, you will have no problem whatsoever in storing this material. You never know, in ten to fifteen years all your effort in storing this material properly from the start may give rise to a valuable resource that another person might be able to use.

If you're using a computer to store all the information you collect, be sure to create separate and appropriate folders for each "type" of information being filed. Don't just stuff everything into the same folder. Always save twice and save often. Save twice in two different locations -- one on the internal hard drive and again on an external device. The zip drive is ideal because of its read/write capability. Also, save under a different file name each time because if your new file becomes corrupted, you still have the one before it and you have only lost what you have done since then. In other words, a first save would be, say "story1" and the next would be, "story2".

'Where and How Do I Generate Ideas?'

Adeline Loh has this piece of advice: "Get out, smell the fresh air and find inspiration from things around you. You can't tell a good story if you don't live life."

Two of the best ways to find ideas for your stories are to "watch the world go by" and "draw on your own experiences".

When you watch the world go by, you are, effectively, observing the people around you. Next time you're waiting at a bus station, airport, train station, supermarket, coffee shop, beach or any public place, look at the people there. Note down their clothes and what they carry with them. Notice their appearance. Listen to what they say and how they say it. Storytellers are often terrible eavesdroppers. We are shameless in listening to people's conversations. It makes any dialogues we create for our stories more authentic and real. As Deanna Mascle says, "Open your heart and your mind and your eyes. We are surrounded by a wealth of wonderful, interesting and challenging stories – more stories than we can tell in ten lifetimes."

Many times, would-be storytellers learn to tell stories based on what they know. This can sometimes be very limiting. A far more useful piece of advice would be if you tell a story based on something you know and, if you don't, make an effort to find out. Never assume that your stories are not important. As Penny Halgren discovered, "What I have come to reali[s]e is that usually what we find boring, others find interesting or helpful."

For example, say you have expert knowledge in teaching English as a second language, your students will really listen to you if you tell them something from your own experience of learning English for the first time. This personal touch makes members of your audience identify with what you say and also bring realism into your story.

Concluding Comments

No doubt, with proper preparation on your part, any research you do will be an effective tool towards helping you become a good storyteller. With the wealth of information that you will gather over time, you will never run out of stories to tell. Let us proceed to the next step where you'll learn an important element of storytelling – the themes of your great story.

STEP 2 - THEMES OF YOUR GREAT STORY

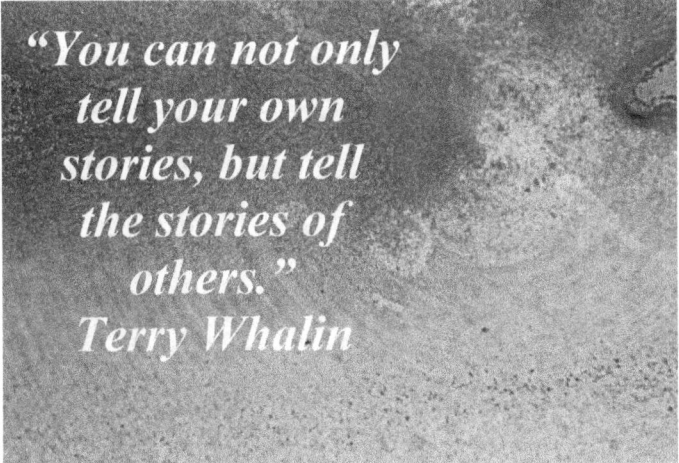

"You can not only tell your own stories, but tell the stories of others."
Terry Whalin

The following is a conversation between an advertising executive and his boss. The boss has just finished going over the executive's masterpiece – a presentation for a client – from cover to cover.

> Executive: So, what did you think of the story I told?
> Boss: Well, it's quite long. I can see you've got an exotic setting and the adventures and so on. It's even an interesting time period. But... what is it about?
> Executive: What do you mean?
> Boss: What is it about?
> Executive: Is it not clear from reading my work?
> Boss: Errr... no.

There's absolute silence for the next two minutes as the Executive thinks of what to say. Then:

Executive: I'll think about it and let you know.

The problem here is easier to understand if the characters in this story were changed, wherein the executive is an aspiring author and the boss an editor. If so, it is a guaranteed fact that the story the executive wrote would be criticised for being haphazard and difficult to follow. In other words, there was no identifiable theme to this story.

> *I think with any story the key is to find the universal, timeless theme that will transcend culture. For example, sibling rivalry is something children of every country can relate to, and if the characters are appealing, and their conflicts are believable, the story will apply across the globe.*
> *Laura Backes*

What is a "theme"?

The only way to salvage such a situation would be for the aspiring storyteller to begin all over again and have theme in place before they begin to tell their story.

What is a theme, though? The Concise Oxford Dictionary defines a theme as 'a subject or topic on which a person speaks, writes or thinks.' It describes a concept and organises a group of repeating ideas. It is often general in nature and unifies all the ideas within the theory. It is the underlying thread of your entire story. There may be sub-themes, but all of them have to be connected to the main theme.

A theme, therefore, is the essence of your story. In other words, the theme is the backbone of your story; it is the frame upon which you add other elements like characterisation, texture, and plot to "flesh" it out.

How Do You Identify A Theme?
The answer lies in asking a simple question: "What is my story about?" What is the message you want your readers to take away from reading your story? Sometimes, the answer to this question can be stated in one sentence; sometimes it has to be explained. Whatever your answer, it has to be clear, concise and precise and encapsulate your entire tale in a few short words. To help you understand what is meant by "a few short words", let's do a short exercise.

Read the following passage aloud. Time yourself:

> From the moment the Nuns were prevented from teaching at the Establishment, the not-wanted-by-any-other-school-teachers were transferred to the premier school. Tika remembered being told, "If you want to know the answers to these questions, come to my tuition class," by one such teacher. Sixteen year-old Tika spent one whole Afternoon working it out. This teacher would teach Nothing at school. And yet, a non-graduate would earn the RM1,200.00 per month. From Afternoon, this teacher would have no more than 25 students a week, 5 students a day for tuition. "One-to-one" They said. At RM400.00 per student, the teacher would get RM120,000.00 cash, tax free every year! This, in addition to the RM14,400.00 as wages. In schools, these beings never taught and days were spent going to school at 7.30 in the morning, playing every available board game. Then at 1.30 p.m. children went home to begin their rounds of tuition – from 3.00 to 5.00, then 5.30 to 7.00 and then 7.30 to 9.30. Nothing about an honest day's work was learnt

from the one set of people who were ideally supposed to take the place of a child's mother at school. Forget trying to complain. One would suffer the same fate as poor Supria had done when Nirmala had thrown her very own tantrum.

This passage if taken from a novel I wrote. And, yes, one of the questions everyone asks is "What's with the use of the capital letters for words like 'Afternoon,' and 'Nothing?'" When I wrote the novel, I was in this phase where I wanted to make words like "afternoon" carry more weight in the story. I digress.

Let us return to the question of time. How long did it take you to read this passage out loud? It took me about a minute and a half to read the passage above. Remember, I am familiar with the story already. How about you? Did you lose interest half-way through? Be honest. There's no harm in saying that you did lost interest, even from the very first sentence.

The reason I chose this paragraph was very simple – I chose something that you would probably never have read before so you would have no clue as to the beginning or the end of this story. You would have had to stop at various places in the paragraph and probably think about what you read. This would have added to the time it took you to read the excerpt and wonder whether or not what you'd read was correct.

The aim of this exercise was to put you in the position of the audience and not the storyteller. As the audience, and after reading that paragraph, I hope that you can understand how difficult it was to understand the message, if any, that was put before you. This is what your audience might face if they have no idea what they're reading when your first tell them your story.

The excerpt you just read has 214 words in it. As a general rule, I have found that when you speak and cannot sustain a person's interest in the first two minutes, you've lost your audience. So it means that you have to capture the interest of your audience with the essence of your story in about 200 words. Bear in mind, as I said previously, the theme of your story can be 200 words, it can be ten. Whatever it is, it must be clearly stated from the moment you start writing. As Janet Kobobel-Grant says, "In our fast-paced world, everyone is looking for a quick way to tell others what a story is about."

Read stories with morals or messages such as children's books to get a feel for what true storytelling is about and develop [your] own unique style of storytelling.
Charles Bonasera

How Do You Choose A Theme?

You have to be very careful how you choose your theme. Nothing could be worse than choosing a theme that is completely out of sync with your audience. A perfect example would be narrating a story about a love gone wrong to someone who is suicidal because his spouse has left him and is, at that moment, standing out on the window ledge of the penthouse of a tall building!

As Jodi Webb says, "Make the personal connection between your reader and your writing. They should want to continue reading because they identify somehow with the characters or theme of your piece. Even if it's about time travelling, vampires taking over Mars, something about it should ring familiar to them – an emotion, a situation, a relationship."

Firstly, you must know who is in audience before you begin telling your story. For instance, if you are telling stories to a group of children, it would be difficult to narrate a tale effectively if your theme is all about the pain that comes from a romance gone wrong. On the other hand, if your audience consists of members of the board of directors for a company, including technical jargon in formulating your theme may not seem too outlandish as they are bound to understand them.

Secondly, you must focus on the keywords you choose. Keywords are words that encapsulate the story you're trying to tell and must have emotional resonance with the audience that you are targeting.

A word of caution: don't push the message or tell the audience how they should feel. If your story is well told and has all the dramatic/emotional elements in the right place, the theme of your tale will shine through. Just give them the facts, information and necessary detail of your story. Be subtle but persuasive when narrating a tale.

Are There Any Examples of Themes?

There are many themes you can choose from to tell your story. The following are some examples of themes:

1. Love will always find a way.
2. Evil lurks where we least expect it.
3. Power corrupts even the purest.
4. Stolen money can only bring misery.
5. There is light at the end of the tunnel.
6. Why fix something that is not broken?
7. Why re-invent the wheel?
8. The end never justifies the means.
9. Beyond love and pain, family is most important.
10. A friend in need is a friend indeed.
11. It is impossible for men and women to be friends.
12. Opportunity seldom knocks twice.
13. Every action has an equal and opposite reaction.
14. Love conquers all.
15. Women love to gossip.

16. No one is beyond redemption.
17. Fairy tales never come true.
18. Dreams always come true.
19. Every law has a loophole.
20. You cannot please everyone.
21. Nothing is more certain than death.
22. Two's a company, three's a crowd.
23. Marriage is for life.
24. Never a borrower or a lender be.
25. It's a small world.
26. Where there's a will, there's always a way.
27. The Mystery of Death.
28. The decline of the American Dream.
29. The blessings of having a family.
30. The evils of racism and slavery.
31. The hypocrisy of a "civilised" nation.
32. Pride comes before a fall.
33. Honesty is the best policy.
34. Wealth spoils the character.
35. Every human being has a father and a mother.
36. Money is the root of all evil.
37. Faith, hope and love; of the greatest of these is love.
38. Spare the rod and spoil the child.
39. Beauty is in the eye of the beholder.
40. All men are born equal.
41. Happiness is but a state of mind.
42. Diamonds are a girl's best friend.
43. When it rains, it pours.
44. One man's meat is another man's poison.

> *[A] would-be storyteller should remember that the best idiom to follow is that the writer must write what the reader wants to read, and not what the writer wants the reader to read. It might sound complicated but if you think about it that's a quite simple philosophy to follow.*
> Brian L. Porter

Let me share with you a trick a lot of storytellers use when they run out of themes; they take a well-used theme and invert it. They challenge the norms and tell their stories effectively. Don't believe me? Let me demonstrate it to you by showing you just how it applies.

Story One
In the modern world, even though man has progressed so much in medicine and technology, the fact remains that it is still the woman who carries a child in her womb for nine months. In one story, this theme is challenged. The theme of this story is about a man who becomes the first ever to become pregnant.

The movie *Junior* centres on a fertility research project wherein a male scientist agrees to carry a pregnancy in his own body. Alex Hesse (Arnold Schwarzenegger) and Larry Arbogast (Danny DeVito) are working on a new drug that will reduce the chances of a woman's body rejecting an embryo and thus causing a miscarriage. When their research funding is withdrawn, and human experimentation is denied them, they decide to test the drug by briefly impregnating Hesse. Hesse, however, becomes attached to his unborn baby.

Story Two
Similarly, it is a widely held belief that a child is born of a man and

woman. However, in the novel *Brave New World*, Aldous Huxley places his tale within a long tradition of books about Utopia, an ideal state where everything is done for the good of humanity as a whole. One of the central themes of his novel is the combination of genetic engineering, bottle-birth, and sexual promiscuity. In his scenario there is no monogamy, marriage, or family. "Mother" and "Father" are obscene words that used only scientifically on rare, carefully chosen occasions to label ancient sources of psychological problems.

Story Three
For over two thousand years, the Christian belief has been that at any given time, a man must by law be married to one woman only and vice versa. In the modern world, in some Muslim nations, a man is allowed up to four wives. This is called polygamy. In an ancient Indian epic, *Mahabharat,* the story is about two warring royal families, the Pandavas and the Kauravas. The Pandavas are five brothers who all shared the same wife, Draupadi - so in this case, one woman had five husbands. *Mahabharat,* though controversial at the time, is still considered by many throughout the world as a great piece of story-telling.

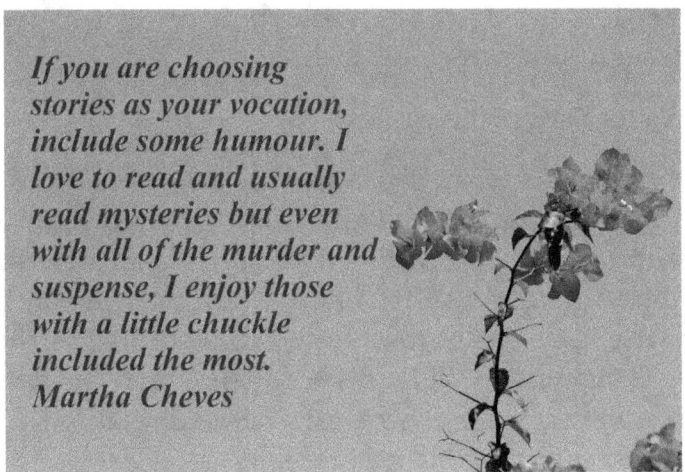

If you are choosing stories as your vocation, include some humour. I love to read and usually read mysteries but even with all of the murder and suspense, I enjoy those with a little chuckle included the most.
Martha Cheves

Flashbacks to Emphasise Your Theme
Another trick that many storytellers use is to start with a flash-

back that immediately showcases the theme in the story. A flashback is an interjected scene that takes the narrative back in time to recount events that happened before the story's primary sequence of events. Many storytellers are cautioned about using a flashback too early on in the story, though. This is because you could lose your audience if you've not set up the main characters and conflict.

I find it impossible to give definite instructions about whether or not to use a flashback in any given story. What I've learnt is that it's easier to first tell the story in a chronological order. Then, when it's completely done, experiment with a flashback by taking a crucial scene and placing it at the beginning of a story. Does it have the impact that you need to engage with the reader.

This is exactly what I did with *The Age of Smiling Secrets.* In one of the earlier drafts, I wrote the entire story in chronological order, beginning in the 1960s and ending in 2005. I could see that the most dramatic moments happened in 1988, 1998 and 2005. I rewrote the first chapter three times starting with these different moments. Then, I chose the one with the most impact and spoke directly to the theme of the tale, which is that no woman should ever have to lose her child, and not in the heart-breaking way that one of the main characters loses hers.

Perhaps Tadeh Daschi puts it best:

> Storytelling is ... an art form that allows us to visuali[s]e and see images through the use of imagination whether it's through spoken word, written form, pictures, paintings, performance etc ... With enough practice, like everything else, it can be easily mastered. But what makes the difference is the visionary lenses through which the storyteller forms the story. It's the vision of the storyteller that brings uniqueness to the finished product.

Concluding Comments

Defining the theme of your story will not only assist you to stay true to your story, it will, in the long run, ensure that your narration of your story will be smoother and ensure that time and energy is not wasted. Let's go on to the next step in this book, which focuses on the reasons for telling your great story.

STEP 3 – THE REASONS FOR TELLING YOUR GREAT STORY

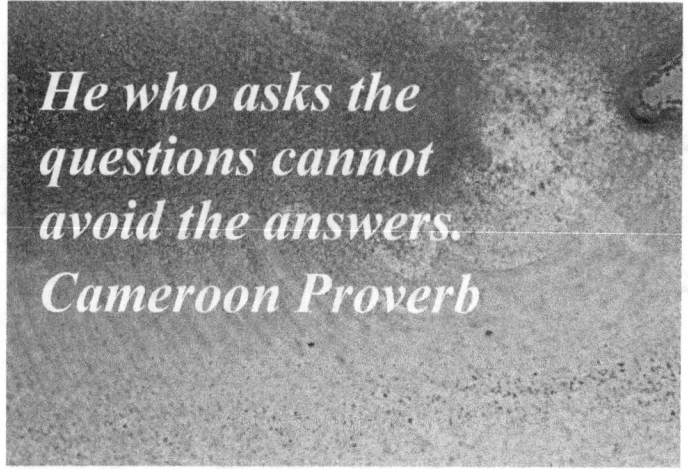

He who asks the questions cannot avoid the answers.
Cameroon Proverb

Have you ever been in the following situation: you are present when the person conducting the meeting is determined to relay the message by telling a story? Any initial excitement at this prospect swiftly disappears because the story he's telling is deadly dull. You wonder why he's telling this story at all. Just as you complete this thought, you look down to stifle a yawn. When you look up, you know that this person has noted your boredom – he avoids making eye-contact with you for the rest of the time. At the end of the meeting, you come to hear from the rest of your colleagues that they too were bored silly by this person's presentation.

The thing is, had the person conducting the meeting asked this very question, "Why am I telling them this story?" no one would have been in this painful situation.

This scenario only serves to demonstrate the importance of getting the basics of storytelling worked out before one begins to tell the story. You see, the reason for telling your great story lies in the questions you ask and there are two important questions you need ask before you can make any story you tell a great story.

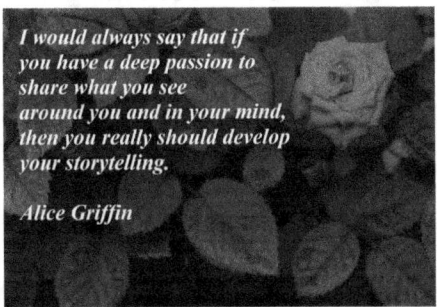

I would always say that if you have a deep passion to share what you see around you and in your mind, then you really should develop your storytelling.

Alice Griffin

Victoria Gregor researched the vocation of storytelling so she could show school administrators and other teachers how valuable teaching storytelling across the curriculum was. Based on her years of experience, research and personal observations on how much storytelling benefitted students, she created a list called, "Forty-Four Reasons for Teaching Storytelling". They are:

1. Aids in strengthening ability to recogni[s]e sequencing details.
2. Benefits the listener as well as the teller.
3. Creates a link between reading skills and writing skills.
4. Creates an opportunity for students to have fun while learning.
5. Develops higher level of comprehension.
6. Develops and strengthens visuali[s]ation skills.
7. Develops an awareness of varied writing styles.
8. Develops awareness of how words affect an audience.
9. Effectively integrates social studies and science into the language arts curriculum.
10. Enhances vocabulary and language development.

11. Enhances development of higher thinking and analytical skills.
12. Enhances ability for identification of main idea.
13. Enhances understanding when tackling unfamiliar text.
14. Fosters the development of creativity.
15. Fosters positive peer interaction and cooperation.
16. Fosters development of self-confidence, pride, poise, and self-esteem.
17. Furnishes a vehicle for the passing on of factual information.
18. Gives teachers insight into their students' feelings.
19. Gives students insight into human behavio[u]r and motives.
20. Helps promote multi-cultural sensitivity and understanding.
21. Introduces effective patterns of language.
22. Is an effective vehicle for teaching and reinforcing curriculum standards?
23. Is a tool for evaluating and capitali[s]ing on a student's strengths?
24. Keeps alive the beliefs and culture of a people.
25. Promotes development of listening skills.
26. Promotes an appreciation for the talents of others.
27. Promotes internali[s]ation of effective writing techniques.
28. Promotes an enthusiasm for learning.
29. Provides an opportunity for students from all reading levels to succeed.
30. Provides for subconscious acquisition and familiarity with narrative patterns.
31. Provides opportunities for self-expression.
32. Provides teachers an opportunity to learn a great deal about student needs.
33. Provides positive sharing experiences for students.
34. Reinforces learning of writing skills.
35. Reinforces and enhances reading skills.

36. Shows the relationship between the written word and spoken word.
37. Skills learned are transferred to other reading and writing activities.
38. Stimulates interest in reading for pleasure.
39. Strengthens the ability for recognition and memory of details.
40. Strengthens sequencing skills.
41. Strengthens analytical skills.
42. Supports and reinforces concepts taught across the curricula.
43. Teaches and reinforces oral skills in all areas of the curriculum.
44. **And most gratifying of all**: Reluctant students who do not feel as competent as their peers and who are considered "losers" by themselves and others, often become the star storytellers. This positive experience turns students around and changes their outlook on what they can accomplish.

[Please note that you may not reproduce the list above or electronically transmit it without permission from Victoria Gregor.]

It is a known fact that telling a story, however ridiculous your story may seem to others, is always an exercise in the power of *your* imagination. No one, absolutely no one, can control what you think. In the words of Joseph Conrad: "Only in men's imagination does every truth find an effective and undeniable existence. Imagination, not invention, is the supreme master of art, as of life."

If you want to think that the world is flat and not a round globe, then, by all means, go ahead. What I will show you in this piece is exactly how to convince others that the world is flat.

You see, the questions we ask determine our thoughts, direct our focus and, thereby, determine the way we think and feel. The answers to these questions help evaluate what things mean. Certain questions can make a difference in people's lives. Once you've followed a proper sequence to asking questions, you'll have that great story.

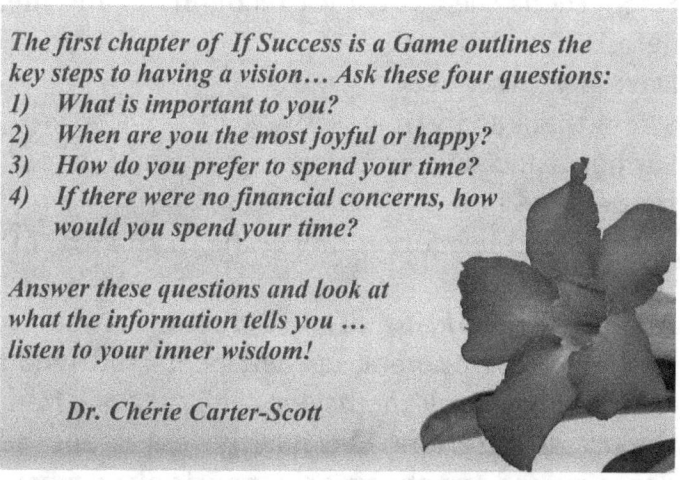

The first chapter of If Success is a Game outlines the key steps to having a vision... Ask these four questions:
1) *What is important to you?*
2) *When are you the most joyful or happy?*
3) *How do you prefer to spend your time?*
4) *If there were no financial concerns, how would you spend your time?*

Answer these questions and look at what the information tells you ... listen to your inner wisdom!

Dr. Chérie Carter-Scott

Why Are Your Telling Your Great Story?
Let us, then, move forward by asking, 'Why are you telling your great story?'
Here's another way to phrase the question: 'What is the purpose of your story?'

As the narrator of a story, you need to answer this question honestly. You need not explain the answer to everyone; indeed, there is no necessity to write the answers down. But you need to explain to yourself, at the very least, why you are embarking on this exercise. It will give you the added confidence and the impetus to continue narrating your tale to the end.

A word of caution: you must not, at any time, feel pressured to produce the *right* answer to this question of 'what is the purpose of your story?' Therein is the beauty of this process. It's the just the process and the structure in which you need to ask these questions that needs to be correct.

Here is an example that showcases why it's important to state the reason you're telling your story. It has to do with the book I co-authored, *Knowledge of Life: Tales of an Ayurveda Practitioner in Malaysia*. My co-author, Vaidya C D Siby, did not state his reason for writing the book in the book itself. Instead, he gave it during his speech at the launch of the book in March 2017. Here's what he said:

> "The idea for this book began more than two years ago [2015]. I had come to a point where I knew I wanted to write a book, but didn't know how to do it. My ideas and theories were all over the place. Who was going to read it? What would its purpose be? Would it really help anyone? Slowly, the answers emerged. My book should help a person who wants to know more about Ayurveda. It should make people aware of its existence and value.
>
> Above all, it should help patients who suffer from illnesses."

Following from this, to give an utterly comprehensive, fool-proof answer, be aware that there are two parts (or rules) to the question of why are you telling this story. They are:
1. Every single person has a different answer to this question.
2. There is no importance cast on whose version is correct but there is a tremendous importance cast on how the storyteller asserts that their own answer is correct.

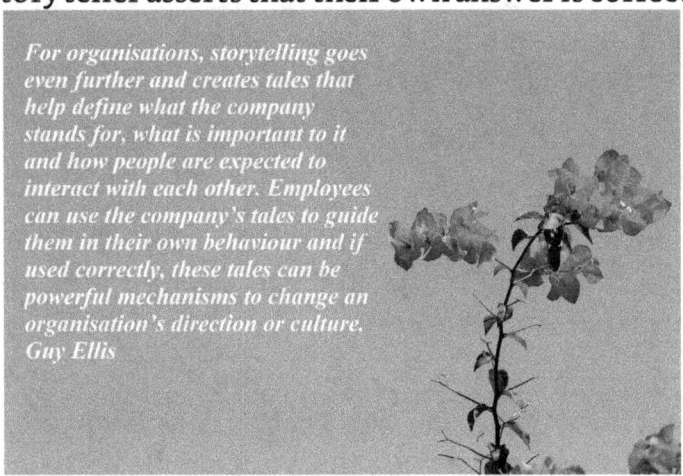

For organisations, storytelling goes even further and creates tales that help define what the company stands for, what is important to it and how people are expected to interact with each other. Employees can use the company's tales to guide them in their own behaviour and if used correctly, these tales can be powerful mechanisms to change an organisation's direction or culture.
Guy Ellis

I've already shown you the importance of the first part of it. Now, let's look at the second one: asserting that your version of the story is correct. Most of us believe that what we see on the news is true and an accurate account of events happening all over the world. For instance, each day there is a portrayal of some war happening in some part of the world.

I recently watched a movie and it was about a war. But, here's the interesting part – the war never happened! It was created in a movie studio using technology because there was a crisis in the leadership of the government. Here's the synopsis of the tale:

> Less than two weeks before Election Day, a scandal erupts that threatens to cripple the President's bid for a second term. But before the incident can cause irreparable damage, a mysterious fixer is called to the White House. The ultimate spin doctor, Conrad Brean has the uncanny ability to manipulate politics, the press and, most importantly, the people. Brean deftly deflects attention from the President by creating a bigger and better story - a war. With the help of Stanley Motss, a famed Hollywood producer and his irreverent entourage, Brean assembles an unlikely crisis team who orchestrate a global conflict unlike any ever seen on CNN.

Isn't that just amazing? A tale spun so well that an entire nation was fooled into thinking there was really a war. What was the name of this movie? *Wag The Dog.*

Now, ask yourself this question: "Why was the movie made at all?"

Might your answer be along the lines of this: the storytellers wanted to examine the blurred lines between politics, media and show-business?

If this is so, can you imagine how powerful this story was? Indeed, after watching this movie, *Wag The Dog,* one begins to wonder whether some of the wars that the world media harp on have actually happened.

The most important implication of asking this question is that the answer you give can influence people to your way of thinking.

It is not my intention to teach you that you should spin tales here – actually, far from it. What I am trying to do is to show you how you can use the power of storytelling to convince others that your ideas and thoughts are correct. It's a matter of telling your story so effectively that yours is the greatest story ever told.

The answer to this question of "Why am I telling this story?" may involve some soul searching on your part. Here are some questions to help you along:

1. Is your story for entertainment purposes?
2. Is telling your story part of your job?
3. Are you telling a story to enter into a competition?
4. Is there are lesson in your story that you're trying to impart to a child?
5. Are you being asked to tell this story against your own wishes to do so?
6. Do you need to tell this story to get what happened in it out of your system?
7. Are you telling a story to inspire others to believe in your cause?
8. Are you telling a story to illustrate a complicated theory you've created?

Here are some possible answers:
- Your story can affect how people think and how they feel.
- It teaches people how to live and practice humanity.
- It gives an idea of what the past was like.
- Alternatively, it shares the view of what's happening in the present moment.
- Your story not only informs people, it helps people makes informed decisions about the various aspects of their lives.

- Your story can teach people to see a different point of view and, therefore, help people co-operate with each other.
- Telling your story can allow people to respond with requisite emotion creatively and through expressive activities.
- Telling your story can help people appreciate the human spirit and the diversity of its expression.
- Telling your story can help people identify and appreciate the cultural, linguistic and spiritual heritage of themselves and others.

The fact remains, though, that these are questions you alone can answer. It is really not difficult to answer any of them. You just need time and patience, and a dose of common sense. For some, the answers come immediately. For others, it takes days. The point to remember is that you have to honest.

As Matt Jones aka Sitting Bear says, "I would tell anyone who wants to venture into storytelling that they need to know and understand the story they are telling. My grandfather told me a long time ago that stories have a spirit and we as the teller give that spirit life and purpose."

What happens when you fail to answer the question "Why am I telling this story?" Well, you'll probably be in the position of the person conducting the meeting in the scenario I described earlier. In other words, you will find that your story will be all over the place by the second sentence you utter or write.

Nevertheless, you may find that even when you have answered the questions above, you're still not satisfied with your answer. But the thing is, at least you're thinking about it and a time will come when you need to answer these questions and you'll have your answers ready.

Here's an example of how this could apply in a business scenario: imagine that you're the head of a fictitious company, Acme Perfumes Inc. This company has created a brand new perfume. As part of the launch, you've agreed to a press conference. You think that with all this publicity, your product is sure to sell. I can guarantee you that one of the first questions an astute reporter will ask you is, "Why did you create this new product?" Will you have an answer prepared?

Now, let me proceed to the next question you will need to answer.

What is the "why" in your story?

When you tell a story, especially if it is to convince someone to agree with the way you perceive things, it is necessary to figure out the "why" in your story.

It is easier to demonstrate this by giving you an example. In my first novel, *The Banana Leaf Men*, the main protagonist is Avantika (Tika, for short). In the story, Tika asks three questions:

- Are women mere commodities?
- Do Indians suffer from an identity crisis?
- Do children who are sent overseas to study return home really "educated"?

Answering these questions is the adventure Avantika embarks on. This was the "why" factor for Tika, and therefore for me as the author. As Tika submitted to the process of the adventure (which in this case was an arranged marriage), she began to find the answers to her questions.

Here's a trick that I used when it came time to publish my latest collection of short stories Two Snakes Whistling at the same time. I used the questions I asked for each story to form the blurb (or material for the 'Back Cover' in publishing lingo). Some of them were:

- Will Divya get into heaven if she writes books for free?
- Why is Mira laughing at her father's funeral?
- Does Tara outgrow her belief that she has three grand-

mothers?

As you can see from the image above that they became part of the blurb for the collection.

When you tell your great story, you are, effectively, putting yourself in the shoes of your main character and answering the questions and dilemmas projected. As Robert Schwartz says, "Feel the story you're telling. An intellectual understanding is all well and good, but stories are truly powerful only to the degree they connect with the reader's heart. You can't connect with your reader's heart unless you feel the story in your own heart."

Would you like to see how this concept is applicable in a business presentation?

Let's go back to our fictitious company, Acme Perfumes Inc. To assist in the marketing of the new product, assume that Acme Perfumes would have had to hire an advertising agency to prepare its advertisements. The person writing the advertisement would have to answer these questions: Why would a potential customer, whether it is a man or a woman, want to buy this perfume? Of what benefit will this perfume be to a potential cus-

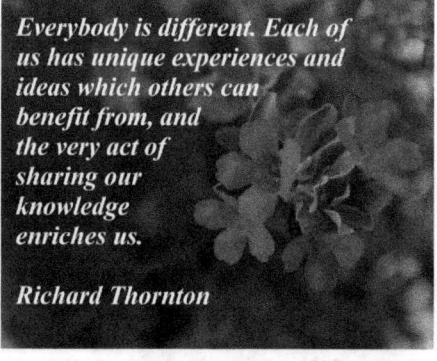

Everybody is different. Each of us has unique experiences and ideas which others can benefit from, and the very act of sharing our knowledge enriches us.

Richard Thornton

tomer?

The advertising executive would have to put himself in the position of a potential customer to understand how to market this product effectively.

Perhaps the answer could be that the perfume would unfold the natural magic of any person wearing it.

Perhaps a man would like to surprise his lady friend with a new present for her birthday.

Perhaps a child would like to buy something special for her mother's birthday.

Whatever the reason, if the advertising executive does his job well, the ad created will tell a story so compelling that the perfume will be an overnight sensation. As Evelyn Clark says

> The Corporate Storytelling system helps organi[s]ations clarify their values, identify their core stories, and fire up their brands. The result is that all the stakeholders - employees, customers, partners, stock owners, peers, and neighbo[u]rs – understand the company's mission better and, in turn, help propel it to greater success.
>
> But in fact, we all can use the same approach in our personal lives as well; it happens all the time. My colleagues in organi[s]ational storytelling and I are actually developing a new paradigm for how people work and live in the 21st Century - and of course, it's based on a practice that's as old as the human race. Social scientists say that human beings are "hard wired" for storytelling.
>
> Stories help us make sense of the world. Our brains readily accept the information in the stories we hear, and then organi[s]e various bits of that information in ways that help us

access those bits when needed.'

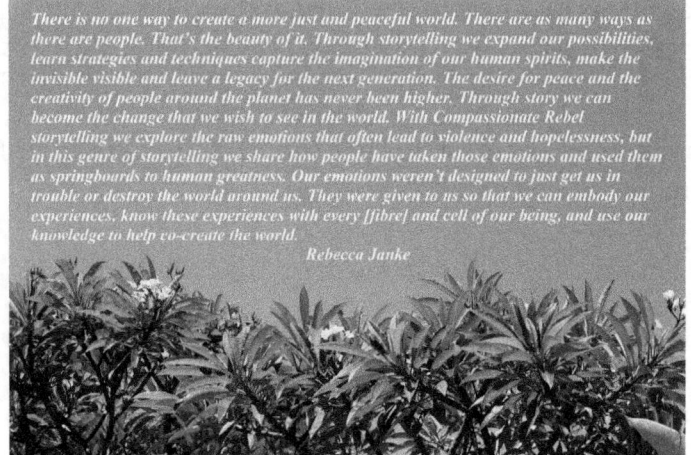

There is no one way to create a more just and peaceful world. There are as many ways as there are people. That's the beauty of it. Through storytelling we expand our possibilities, learn strategies and techniques capture the imagination of our human spirits, make the invisible visible and leave a legacy for the next generation. The desire for peace and the creativity of people around the planet has never been higher. Through story we can become the change that we wish to see in the world. With Compassionate Rebel storytelling we explore the raw emotions that often lead to violence and hopelessness, but in this genre of storytelling we share how people have taken those emotions and used them as springboards to human greatness. Our emotions weren't designed to just get us in trouble or destroy the world around us. They were given to us so that we can embody our experiences, know these experiences with every [fibre] and cell of our being, and use our knowledge to help co-create the world.

Rebecca Janke

Concluding Comments

People tell stories for many reasons. For some, like novelists, just the act of telling a story is what they love to do. Other people tell stories to get their points across and achieve an objective. No matter what the purpose, it is important to remember that you must learn to identify both with your audience and with the people in your story – this is the subject matter of the next chapter.

STEP 4 - IT'S ALL ABOUT THE PEOPLE

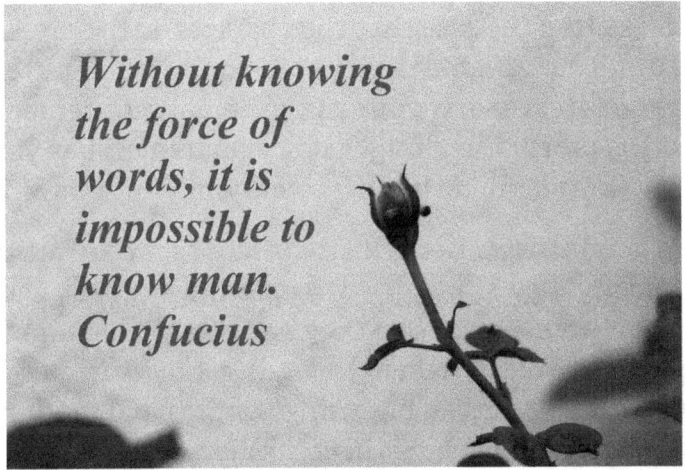

Without knowing the force of words, it is impossible to know man.
Confucius

Let's take this example: you're an executive in a corporation and need to make a presentation about the company's newest product to potential investors. The product is a new line of perfumes for women. You go out of your way to explain all of this and think that you can convince your boss by telling a story.

You realise that you've failed in this when, at the end of your presentation, your boss says, "I'm sorry, but I think you don't understand that the product is for a *woman*, not a man."

Have you ever read a story in which the characters were almost identical? They had names like Bill and Billy and throughout the tale you wondered, "Who are they talking about now? Bill or

Billy?" One of the most obvious examples of this is Shakespeare's play *Twelfth Night* where there were two characters, Olivia and Violet. It is common to for those who appreciate the play to get them confused.

Which character comes to mind when I mention the story *Gone with the Wind*? Was your answer Scarlet O'Hara or Rhett Butler? Good. Now, let me ask you, who *wrote* the novel *Gone with the Wind*? Chances are that while you know every character in the story, you would have to think twice before you answered that the author of this book is Margaret Mitchell.

You see, it is often the case that the characters that are unique in a tale are more memorable that the storyteller – long after you've narrated your great story, your audience will not remember the details of the story. They might not even remember you. However, they *will* remember the characters you've portrayed.

You see, a good storyteller tells their tale as if they are painting a masterpiece. They start off with an empty canvas and slowly add colour; with every stroke they add to the character of their masterpiece. Similarly, when you tell a tale, imagine you are painting on a blank canvas, but using words to paint your picture and portray the human beings in your tale.

Who are you talking about? Is it a man or a woman? Is it an adult or a child? Is he Indian, Chinese, Malay, Hispanic, African-American? Is he old or young? Is this person alive? Sometimes, when the narrator is hopeless, you would not even have the answers to these basic questions.

Whether you are referring to a fictitious person or someone who is real, the singular rule that applies to them both is this: Your aim should be to create individuals who leap off the page.

The person whose story you're narrating must exude energy and have a dramatic impact. They must at all times be more exciting and grab our attention more than the ordinary people we meet each day. Your characters can be larger than life. They must be able to cope with momentous things that are about to happen to them. They must be characters we can identify with. Nick Daws goes further and advises, "Choose your viewpoint character carefully. Once you know this character, you will find that other ingredients of the story – dialogue, setting and so on – fall into place much more easily. Even with a one-page short story, you should be able to see your viewpoint character clearly in your mind before you start writing."

How do you do all this? It's not difficult. You just have to take it step-by-step.

Let's start with the first point: the people in your story must be believable.

A character who is realistic might be someone you can identify with like a parent, sibling or so on. They might be someone who exists in real life.

However, there are characters that are not realistic at all. For example, Superman, Count Dracula, Mary Poppins and so on are not characters we're likely to meet in life. They are too extreme or too extraordinary to be real. But you can believe in them because they have recognisably human characteristics. You believe in their cause, in what they do, what their aspirations are. You can identify with them.

In tales like *Superman*, the storyteller was able to paint his masterpiece so well that Clark Kent's personality comes through. It's as if he's alive.

What's the trick behind this ability to create believable characters? The trick is to give the characters you portray an individual personality; give them quirks, mannerisms, an individual style of speaking or thinking and a clear motivation. Make them three-dimensional. Make your characters strong, sometimes ruthless and determined. Audiences absolutely love characters who are in positions of influence and authority; or indeed those who achieve their aims despite being the underdog.

The ability to make your characters believable is only limited by your own imagination. Each characteristic of your hero or heroine must be portrayed so clearly that people will say, "I could see this character right before my very eyes".

How do you do this? It's quite simple: observe an individual. Observe his personality and within moments, you'll be able to capture his quirks, his mannerisms, and other habits. This is nothing to be ashamed of. Remember, you're only using these people as templates for creating a character, not writing about the person themselves. The idea is not to use so much of any one person that he recognises himself in your words and accuses you of defaming him.

Do not get your characters all mixed up. When telling a story where the word count is in the thousands, it can get complicated. I use a simple formula to record all of the information about a character. It helps me to expand my imagination and also to make the characters more real. I call it "Character Profiling". I list down the following about people:

- Name
- Date of Birth
- Place of Birth
- Age at the time the story is written
- Gender
- Distinguishing features
- Background
- Main Character Trait
- Significant Events that have happened in this person's life
- Appearance: Hair, Eyes, Complexion, Height/Build, Skin Colour
- Hobbies
- Habits

- What does he or she like to do in their spare time?
- What does s/he dislike most in life?
- Relationships with their family
- Relationships with their friends
- Where has she lived in her life
- Does he like pets? If so, what kind?
- Strengths
- Weaknesses
- Problems
- What motivates this person?

Completing this, even if it is only in your head, will provide you with an enormous amount of useful background information about a character and their life. It will make it easier when you are trying to narrate a story about this person or even something remotely related to them.

If you think that these rules only apply to fiction, you're mistaken. Try this – let's go back to our perfume company. Say the person you are trying to portray is a woman and the name of the perfume is Jasmine. Here's some of the information you can record about her:

- Name – Jasmine Bloggs
- Date of Birth – 4th of July 1975
- Place of Birth – Canada
- Age at the time the story is written - 31
- Gender - Female
- Distinguishing features – she has grey eyes
- Background – she hails from a relatively poor but pious background. As a child, her father would take her to Church every Sunday. Her father has since passed away and she has moved to the city. There are no jasmine trees in the city.
- Main Character Trait – she's a generous person.
- Significant Events that have happened in this person's life – first person in her family to graduate from college.

- Appearance: Long and dark brown hair; grey eyes; clear complexion; average build; skin the colour of honey
- Hobbies – singing
- Habits – bad habit of smoking.
- What does she like to do in her spare time? – embroidery
- What does she dislike most in life? – dishonesty
- Relationships with her family – after her father dies, she has no family to speak of as she was an only child and her mother died in childbirth.
- Relationships with her friends – pleasant.
- Does she like pets? If so, what kind? – does not mind dogs but hates cats.
- Strengths – believes that people have to have a balance in their lives – they have to work hard as well as play hard.
- Weaknesses – smokes
- Problems – does not have much money. From time to time she indulges in small luxuries.

When telling the story, imagine how effective it would be with all these little details woven into the tale. When making a presentation, rather than just saying, "We have a new product. It should appeal to women of all ages," imagine the impact if you said something like this:

> Jasmine was humming a soft tune. Then, on an impulse, she snuffed out her cigarette, threw it in the dustbin and walked into the shopping mall. When she reached one of the kiosks, a woman presented her with a beautiful bottle in the shape of a bud. The memories came flooding in – Jasmine remembered how, as a child, she would hold her father's hand with her right one and clutch a whole bunch of jasmine buds in her left. They would go to church together each Sunday and after the service she would place some of the jasmine on her mother's grave. She knew that when her father chased the cats that sat around her mother's grave, it was more a show on his part to hide the tears in his grey eyes – how much they

both missed her mother. Jasmine sighed deeply. Here she was, in the city, alone and just about making ends meet. Still, on this summer day, her birthday, she just had to get that perfume for herself and reached out to buy a bottle of the jasmine scent.

The presentation would have taken no more than ten minutes, but just imagine its impact.

In Appendix C, I've added this Character Profile which you can print any number of times and use for your benefit.

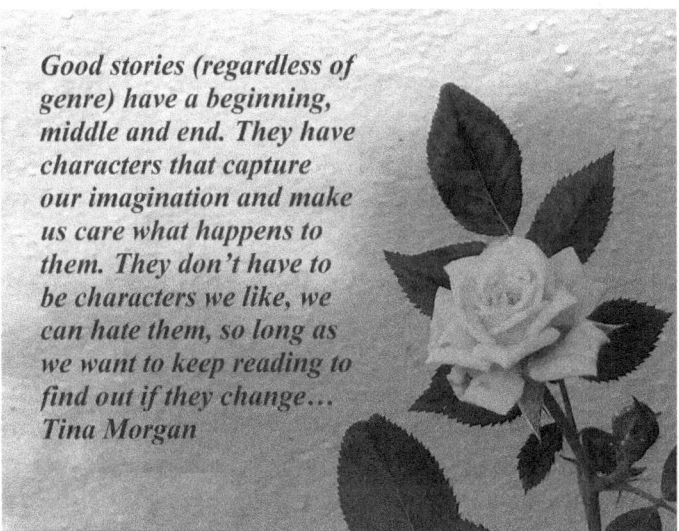

Good stories (regardless of genre) have a beginning, middle and end. They have characters that capture our imagination and make us care what happens to them. They don't have to be characters we like, we can hate them, so long as we want to keep reading to find out if they change...
Tina Morgan

Choosing the Right Name for Your Characters

This issue is often overlooked, but is one of the most important in any story you tell. You can suggest a tremendous amount about a person's age and background by the name he/she has. It is a well-known fact that all names have popular connotations and associations to which the reader subconsciously attaches an image. For example, in the West, Bert is an easy going person, but make him Albert and you get an image of a pedantic, middle-class gentlemen – a barrister, perhaps. Then there are the upper-class English names like Horace and William. Give your character a name like

Justin and it immediately conjures up a young man. If in doubt, stick with Biblical names like Matthew, Mark, Luke, John, Rebecca, Ruth and so on.

At this point you might be saying, "This is generalising things in the extreme," but this is what storytelling is all about. You're not telling a story that will appeal to one person alone but you're appealing to the general public. So, there's no harm in being general.

Now, let me share with you some generalisations from my area of the world. As each city becomes increasingly multi-cultural, it might be to your advantage to have some Asian characters in your story. If you give a character a name like Rita Berganza, one immediately conjures the image of a Parsi lady. Give a name like Patel and one would associate it with a person who originates for north India as those in the south rarely have this name. Give a person a surname like Menon, Nair or Pillay and more often than not, he's a Malayalee and hails from the state of Kerala. For male characters, it is safe to use names like Ashok or Raj – they're quite common names for men from both North and South India. Common names for girls are usually Asha and Maya. For the Chinese, names like Lim, Chan and so on are fine. For ladies, the standard is May-May.

What about pets or animals in your story? Instead of choosing the more boring ones like Max, Sandy or Boxer, try to observe the names people give their pets. Who can forget Faussette, Napoleon's dachshund? Or Karl Lagerfeld's cat, Choupette? I had friends who absolutely loved coffee and named their cats Mocha and Chino. Then there's Zazu and Mufasa from The Lion King. None fascinates me more than the piglet that was named Chris. Certainly, there was nothing unique about Chris, until its owner gave us his full name – Chris P Bacon.

When it came to naming the pets in my stories, I looked no further that my dog, Ladoo. Indeed, that's the title for a collection of stories about my dachshund – *Ladoo Dog: Tales of a Sweet Dachshund*. When it came time to use it in my novel, though, I 'upgraded' the spelling to a the more commonly used word for an Indian sweetmeat – Laddoo.

Things Don't Always Go to Plan

Things don't always go to plan, though, when giving names to your characters. When I wrote my novels, like many writers, I looked at my background to draw inspiration. In *The Age of Smiling Secrets*, there are two characters, S P Mama and Papa Aunty. I loved those names and though that they were quaint. When I sent off the manuscript to be edited by someone in the UK, I was deeply disheartened when she wrote back criticising me for the names I'd chosen.

You see, S P Mama and Papa Aunty were derived from the names my grandmothers used to be called. S P Mama was from Amma and Papa Aunty was from Papa. Papa is the Tamil word for baby girl and many a Tamil child will be called 'Papa'. I still remember her exact words: "The British reading public will not be able to get their head around a woman being called Papa."

I must admit that I was so angry at the time that I wondered if the British reading public were, indeed, that stupid. Couldn't they understand a culture not their own? After I'd calmed down, I made the decision to stick with these names because I figured that readers would appreciate such cultural differences and the authenticity of my tale. And they did.

[S]tories are at their best when they focus on the characters, their agendas, obstacles and how they go about resolving their problems or gaining enlightenment.
Rob Parnell

What Motivates Your Character?

One way to make your characters come to life is to "look inside" and figure out what makes them tick. What motivates them? Every single person has something that drives them; a force that propels them forward. It can be the desire to be loved, wanting to look after those you care about or trying to gain a mastery over something so as to garner the approval of others. It could even be a desire to seek justice for a wrong done. Whether the motivation is good or bad, it's this motivation that shapes our characters' personalities, and affects their attitudes and actions.

Once you understand what motivates your characters, you'll know not only who they are as individuals but how they'll behave in any given situation. This is important for one reason only – it will help your audience decide whether or not they like this character. A man who holds an entire hospital hostage because he is extorting money from a doctor may not be liked. But, a man who holds an entire hospital hostage so that his son will be given treatment may be seen in sympathetic light.

Here's an example I often use to explain how to express the motivation of your character: think of your story in terms of a trial in a courtroom. You are the lawyer for the prosecution. Your audience is the jury and your main character in the tale is the defendant. It always begins with the lawyer for the prosecution making an opening statement. Then, the lawyer for the defence makes his statements. Thereafter, the "scene of the crime" is explored in detail by one party. When the prosecution's finished, you switch to the viewpoint of the defence. Once the case is completed, the jury makes up their mind and comes to a conclusion about the so-called crime your character has committed.

If you find this method hard, then I'll give you another one to help you along: ask yourself these simple questions and the answer to them will be what motivates your character.

- What does this character want?
- Why does this character want that?
- Who or what stands in the way of this character getting it?

These questions can help you figure out what is at stake for your character, what they stand to gain or lose, and why it is important to them. If you know the answers to those questions and you've communicated them to your audience, then you don't have much to worry about.

Contrast Your Characters
Ensure that your characters are as different from each other as possible and, without doubt, you'll have an explosive story. Also, the more contrast there is, the less the chances your audience will mix them up. Most importantly, do not give characters similar names – never give the audience the chance to ask, "Wait! Does she love Harry or Hugh?"

Concluding Comments
By using all of the different ways in which you can distinguish your characters, you can guarantee that when you tell your story it will not only be vivid, it will also be interesting and motivated. In addition, the story will be memorable, and perhaps, you too, as the storyteller, will be equally remembered.

STEP 5 – PAINT YOUR SETTING

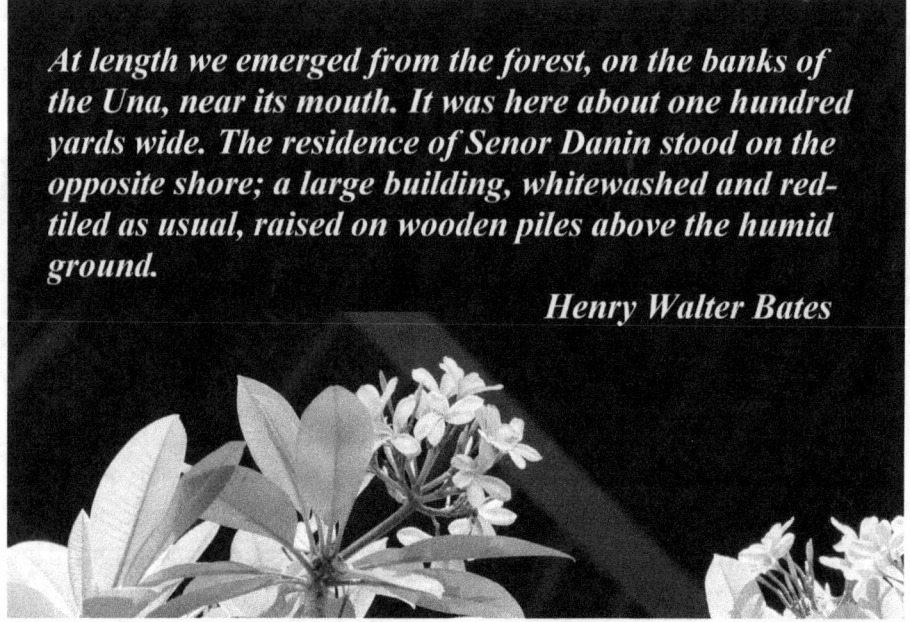

At length we emerged from the forest, on the banks of the Una, near its mouth. It was here about one hundred yards wide. The residence of Senor Danin stood on the opposite shore; a large building, whitewashed and red-tiled as usual, raised on wooden piles above the humid ground.

Henry Walter Bates

Look at the quote above.

I once observed a trial for manslaughter. Briefly, a woman was found dead near a mangrove and her husband was accused of the murder. There were two witnesses to the crime. The first witness gave the following testimony:

"Yeah. I was there. It was near the creek." Effective - short and sweet; perhaps even somewhat convincing.

The second witness had this to say:

"There was no moon that night. So, it was very dark. We had just finished dinner and were driving back home. The wind was blowing and I could smell the rain. But, as we came near the creek, I saw an abandoned car by the side of the road and I knew there was something else. There was a smell of blood as well; you know how blood smells rusty? I told my husband to stop the car. He refused but I insisted. When we alighted, I walked past the other car and the front part of it was still hot. The rain started to pour and we were just about to leave when I heard the scream."

Can you guess which testimony was more interesting to listen to? Indeed, which testimony was likely to avoid a case of the judge falling asleep?

Notice how engaging the second testimony is. This is to show you that the skills you learn in storytelling, which people often push aside as creative writing skills, can be applied to everyday situations.

> *The pleasure is in the storytelling... Allow your characters to come alive, make your setting real, and like a good actor – "deliver" every line until the end.*
>
> *Nadine Laman*

There are numerous settings you can pick from to make your story come alive. If your story is about the dangers of claustrophobia, then tell a tale about people who are trapped in small, frustrated lives. Give them a life that is not restricted but where rules and conventions keep them penned in. If you wish to talk about freedom and fighting for it, then my advice would be to paint a scene that is sweeping and colourful. In other words, make the setting of your scene reflect the mood and feel of the book. Use it to build the atmosphere of your story.

With reference to the witnesses' testimonies above, the techniques employed by the second witness to describe the setting can be divided into four parts, namely:
- the elements
- the senses
- the settings
- atmosphere

Let's look at each one of these in some detail.

The elements
Xenocrates of Chalcedon was a student of Plato who went on to become head of the Academy. He was an early believer in atomic theory and originated the classical distinction between mind, body and soul. Xenocrates writes in the following terms:

> Thus he then classified living creatures
> into genera and species, and divided them in every way
> until he came to their elements,
> which he called the five shapes and bodies,
> aither, fire, water, earth and air.

[*aither* being ether]

These very elements of ether, fire, water, earth and air can be used to describe any scene you wish to portray. Read the following passage and see if you can identify the elements the author mentions:

> When it happened, the earthquake jolted the Earth's rotation. This was enough to trim a couple of microseconds off the clock. It seems a small amount of time, yes, especially in the history of Earth where whole continents have been known to disappear in mere minutes. However, this little seismic bump was enough to displace trillions of tons of

water in a few seconds. The water pushed outward at the speed of a jet plane but no one heard this. Indeed, it was invisible. Only, when it neared the shores, the speed slowed and huge waves formed. By the time it hit the shores, this tsunami brought with it a destruction of unparalleled disaster.

Adapted from *Tide of Grief*
http://www.msnbc.msn.com/id/6777595/site/newsweek/?ng=1

Use as many senses as you can with your language, shine a light in dark corners, create harmony or temporary discord [underpinned by a sound motive] with your words, grip the reader. Smell and taste success.
Jack Stewart

The senses

Have you ever just wanted to converse with someone and found that you have nothing to say? Are your answers just monosyllabic? Would you like to be a more engaging conversationalist? Here's a very simple way in which you can do this. Read this paragraph and you'll see just what I mean:

> I am in the Kuala Lumpur International Airport waiting for someone to arrive. I begin to observe things around me. What I notice is this: the colours featured most in here are silver and blue because of the steel frames and the marble flooring. I know that one of the trees outside produces the jasmine flowers but I cannot smell them. All I hear are people speaking English with American accents. The taste of the

coffee is strong as it is from one of the many "imported" outlets like San Francisco Coffee or Coffee Bean. The air-conditioning must be set on 'High' because I'm freezing!

Can you identify the senses that I have written about in the above paragraph?

- The colours featured most in here are silver and blue because of the steel frames and the marble flooring – refers to the **sense of sight**.
- I know that one of the trees outside produces the jasmine flowers – refers to **the sense of smell**.
- All I hear are people speaking English but with American accents. – refers to the **sense of hearing**.
- The taste of the coffee is strong as it is from one of the many "imported" outlets like San Francisco Coffee or Coffee Bean. – refers to the **sense of taste**.
- The air-conditioning must be set on "High" because I'm freezing! – refers to the **sense of touch**.

Yes, they are the five senses of sight, smell, taste, hearing and touch. These five senses can help you paint the picture of your setting. A common rule of thumb is that the more unusual the location of your story, the more exciting your story.

Here is very useful advice given by John Ling:

> What most people don't reali[s]e is that stories are not movies. To put this into perspective, real life is three-dimensional, movies are two-dimensional (having sight and sound), and stories are one-dimensional (having only words). In fact, the only medium that is closest to storytelling is radio. If you have ever listened to the old dramas and mysteries put out by broadcasters such as the BBC, you will notice how vivid they are despite their minimal description. They rely only on dialogue and sound effects. Therefore, if you rely on sight, your stories will end up being very flat. A solution is to use what novelist John Barth called

triangulation. Triangulation suggests that you should cut down on sight, and focus on other senses such as smell, hearing and touch. You will get a well-rounded story this way... There is a very practical reason for this. In the past, before the advent of film and photography, writers were expected to travel far and wide and bring back vivid descriptions. This is understandable, since most people lacked exposure in those days. But in today's multimedia world, I don't know anyone who doesn't know how an African savannah looks like, or Venice, or the Himalayas.

The settings

The following are various settings you can think about when telling your story:

1. Menacing

This always comes into play when telling an adventure story, a thriller, a horror tale or crime story. Your setting must be hostile. The key words here should be danger and excitement. Examples of these would be desolate deserts, towering mountain ranges, crashing seas, thunder and lightning, typhoons and so on.

Another way is to create an illusion – what this means is where you choose a normal looking setting and then narrate a story that shows that this normal setting isn't really that normal after all!

Then, apply these to the situation you are trying to tell. For example, in a boardroom situation, you could say, "... the air in the boardroom was electrifying. No one dared to speak and the only sound was the low din of the industrial air conditioning."

2. Glamour

I'm pretty sure that at some point in your life you've wondered, "Just how do the rich and famous live?" I would like to think that, conversely, those born rich must wonder, "What is it like to be poor?" The point I'm trying to make is that these are the situations you can think of when you need to create your story. Here are some samples of glamorous occupations: pilots, TV presenters, footballers, fashion models, heart surgeons, pop stars, corporate lawyers and bodyguards.

3. Power

As the saying goes, "Power corrupts". What better setting can you pick than where the powerful people congregate and operate like company boardrooms, government departments, casinos, back-street-places and old boys clubs, to name a few.

4. Workplaces

These are what I call "breeding grounds" for great stories to narrate. Take a legal firm - the office-politicking, the in-house romances, the wheeling and dealing, the clients are **all** dramas just waiting for you to create a story. Pick a hospital – the nurses' romances with the doctors, the failed operations, the anxiety patients go through from treatments endured, the grief suffered by those who have to fetch the bodies of the dead from the mortuary... all these are just fascinating tales in the making. Think about it, what do animators do? What is it like being a doctor or a crime scene investigator? What does a computer graphics designer's office look like? What interesting stories can an architect tell me about the houses he builds? Do you get the idea?

5. Science Fiction

Of all settings, this is the most exciting one because you can create the most bizarre setting and yet people will believe you. The only limit is your imagination.

When your audience listens to your story, they are most captivated when you transport them to an exotic, unusual or glamorous location. Whether or not it is a beach on a deserted island or a murderer's cell, where your story is set enhances the entire feature of your story. What you must aim for is this: through the words you use to narrate your stories, your reader must feel himself transported to a strange and exotic land full of unusual and intriguing customs and traditions. Your audience must feel that they are there – down every dusty road, every sun-kissed beach and so on. If you choose a place that does exist, make sure that you know the history of the place you have created well enough.

A story should touch all our sense and emotions when possible. I want to laugh, cry, worry and care – all that makes us human.
Bill Blake

If you live in London, you may assume that everyone knows what London is like and therefore there is no need to set your story there. This would be a mistake. Your view of London will be completely different from someone else's view of London. The trick here is to make your narration sound so exciting that people will want to visit London again, just to see London through your eyes. Your audience will be forming their own personal picture of how your world will look like in their own heads.

A word of warning though: although you should be descriptive, you should not narrate a travelogue. Always keep in mind that the setting is your backdrop, not the main story.

Atmosphere

There is no doubt that when you describe a place, the atmospheric images you create can enhance your story. For example, you say "I went to my office today."

There's nothing amiss in this sentence, but there's nothing exciting in it. There's nothing in the sentence to tell the reader whether you're happy or sad; nothing to say if you had a great day or a most unproductive one; nothing exciting.

Now, say this: "I went to my dingy office today." Immediately, your audience will picture a gloomy, cramped and perhaps backstreet room. There are files all over the place. One battered filing cabinet, a rickety old desk and the only thing stopping it from toppling over is the paper pushed under one leg. The impression people get of you is that you're frustrated in your job. You're miserable and wish to get out.

Now, say this: "I went to my spacious office today." Immediately, your audience thinks that your office is bright, modern, well-staffed, buzzing and the telephone lines are constantly ringing. You're successful in your job. Relatively happy and enjoy your work.

See how just one adjective changed the whole perception your audience had both about you and your story?

Similarly, use adverbs and you'll be able to manipulate and alter the thinking of your audience. If Mary struggled to open the front door, then she's probably lost her key. If Mary's frantically struggling to open the front door, she's probably in danger of some sort.

The point about atmosphere is that it helps to change the mood of the place you're trying to describe.

For instance, say you're trying to sell an item that will promote security. Ideally, you should describe the scene using words that have an ominous effect – howling winds, stormy nights, dark clouds, pouring with rain, grey skies, thunder and lightning.

The Magic That Is Psychic Distance

In 2013, I signed up for a self-edit course with Writers Workshops. I once interviewed its owner/founder, Harry Bingham. During this self-edit course, I learnt one of the most important lessons any storyteller can ever master – the magic that is psychic distance. I cannot explain this any better than Emma Darwin can. I would urge you to read her full blog post called 'Psychic Distance: what it is and how to use it' (https://emmadarwin.typepad.com/thisitchofwriting/psychic-distance-what-it-is-and-how-to-use-it.html) That said, here is a summary of the basic premise of psychic distance.

Psychic Distance is also called Narrative Distance because, basically, it's about where the narrative (and therefore the reader) stands, relative to a character. It can be broken down in the following way:

Psychic 1: It was winter of the year 1853. A large man stepped out of a doorway.
It is remote and objective. The narrator is very much in charge, telling us a lot about where we are and what's happening: it's all about information and context.

Psychic 2: Henry J. Warburton had never much cared for snowstorms.
It is bringing in some particulars: the narrator is telling us (informing us) about a place, and an individual group or person, and something about their emotions or personality.

Psychic 3: Henry hated snowstorms.
It is more particular: the narrator's voice is beginning to show us (evoke for us) the particular character and their experience.

Psychic 4: God how he hated these damn snowstorms.
It is beginning to colour the voice of the narrator with the vocabulary and point-of-view of the character.

Psychic 5: Snow. Under your collar, down inside your shoes, freezing and plugging up your miserable soul.
It is tight close-up and subjective: almost a brain download, with thoughts and sensory information all jumbled up.

Concluding Comments

However well you construct your tale, with a theme in place, a plot that is carried through to its end and characters that positively sizzle with energy, if the setting is not properly conveyed the story you tell will seem a little 'lost'. It is the setting that grounds a story and gives it a strong foundation.

STEP 6 - JOIN THE DOTS

> *We are what and where we are because we have first imagined it.*
> *Donald Curtis*

A crucial part of storytelling is plotting. When you plot your tale, you're constructing the story to appear in a logical narrative, with a balance of action and drama. It helps you to explain how to plan out the predicament and upsets that your characters face and how to offer them a solution to the problem. Once you've mastered the basics of plotting you'll need to put your story into a coherent structure. To help you, let's look at what's called the Three Act Drama.

The Three Act Drama.

In Act 1 you start at the beginning. In the first part of your tale you will have to do the following:

- Introduce the main character and establish who he or she is.
- Introduce the rivals and the conflict.
- Show what is at stake.
- Paint your backdrop by setting the time and location of your story.
- Introduce your theme.
- The Inciting Event (the thing that kick-starts the action).

In Act 2 you catch your breath. Some of the things to do at this point are to enhance the themes –develop them a little. Perhaps you can show the different views of a particular theme here or even the "thinking" process; one view can be interpreted by different people in different ways. In addition, you will also need to move the action on and have several incidents that create more tension for your readers. One technique that many storytellers employ is called 'reversal of expectation' – what this means, effectively, is that you create an incident/scene that makes you reader change his mind about a particular character or situation.

In Act 3 you will have to quicken the pace a little. To keep your audience wanting more, you should make the ending one that demands immediate action. You will also find a suitable resolution for your characters' dilemmas and tie up any loose ends. You need to make sure that the end of your story strikes the right balance between satisfaction for your reader and continuing enthusiasm.

Perhaps one of the most dramatic ways in which you can end your story is to have it echo the beginning of your story. Example – in the beginning of your story, your main character is scared of snakes. Now in this final chapter, he needs to get to the centre of an old ruin to rescue his lady-love as she has been kidnapped and is being held hostage. But his path is blocked by a nest of snakes and he has to overcome his fear. He has to conquer his phobia and inner demons.

At this point, many people may say that this applies to the field of creative writing. However, as Gail Trahd has pointed out, "Online sales letters, if they are written well, are stories. They are stories that keep the reader reading until the very last sentence."

Take a typical sales letter you would prepare for a product and see how the Three Act Drama features in your sales letter:

Part 1 - Act 1
- Headline and Sub-headline –

These are intended to immediately capture the interest of your reader – the hero in this three act drama.
- Introduce the problem - relate to the reader and explain product – this is the part where the hero's main conflict and all that is at stake to him are stated.
- Who is the note from and establishing the author's credibility – these are the ingredients of which the main characters in this drama are - you and your reader!

Part 2 - Act 2
- Detail the benefits and features of the product – Here, the hero catches his breath by trying to understand the product in a little more detail.... But not for too long

Part 3 – Act 3
- See how the first thing the sales letter states after the benefits and features have been expanded upon is always a sentence like: "You've just made it in time to take part in this offer ..." Is this not an example of quickening the pace of the three act drama?
- Then there are the bonuses and the guarantee - these are always the part where the loose ends of the story are tied up. For example, "Yes, you will have the eBook to tell a great story but if you get into trouble, we will always be there to help you! You will have unlimited email access for 30

days."
- Then it is time for the close of the story - the hero is asked to make the decision.

"Download Now"

"Invest in your future Now"

Now do you understand why people in marketing always insist that you must tell a story to sell? It makes it appeal to the reader on a personal level. Your readers (or in this case, those who are investing in your product or services) will believe what you say and follow you.

Let's go back to the basics.

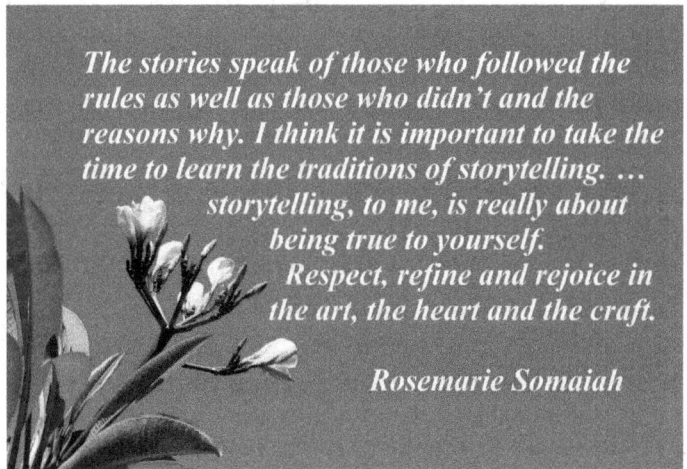

The stories speak of those who followed the rules as well as those who didn't and the reasons why. I think it is important to take the time to learn the traditions of storytelling. ... storytelling, to me, is really about being true to yourself. Respect, refine and rejoice in the art, the heart and the craft.

Rosemarie Somaiah

Steps to Plotting
There are three basics steps to follow when you plot your story.

Step 1 – Writing to A Formula
There are books written on this topic alone. To start, let's look at some of the more common formulae. Where it's applicable, I'll give an example in an advertising context, in particular, advertising on the television.

The most popular of all of is **the quest**. What this means is that a problem crops up, the main character's life is suddenly turned upside down and he has go in search of a solution.. Solving this problem will test the main character to the limit physically, emotionally and intellectually. There are forces beyond his control which make things difficult for him.

The second formula is that of **the prize**. There is not necessarily an element of danger in this but instead there is an ambition or goal that needs to be achieved. But, success is not at all likely as this person does not have even the basic ingredients for success.

Let me give you an example of a storyline using this formula of "the prize" this in business terms. You work in a company that's just launched a new product. It is aimed a helping girls who suffer from acne. You have been given the task of advertising this product. Here's a simple storyline to help you understand how the plot of your story might appear.

The ultimate prize for this girl would be to attend a party. Only several things are in her way:
1. She does not like what she looks like as she suffers from acne.
2. There are only two weeks to the party and even if she could, this is not enough time to improve her skin.
3. Then, a fairy godmother brings her this magic cream; lo and behold, her skin clears in time for the party.

The race is the third formula you can use to tell your story. An obvious example is a race across the globe to be the first to reach the finish point to win the $1,000,000.00 prize. Your story could also involve a race between rivals for a love interest, or for a scientific discover. In business terms, this is the technique used by all people who know that there are two or more of the same kinds of products in the market.

The puzzle is one that is used to assist people unravel a mystery. Solving the problem is at the heart of the story and is used by most detective and crime mystery writers.

If all else fails, there is one formula that is time-tested you can always rely on – **romance**. The formula is simple – boy meets girl; boy loses girl; boy wins her back (or vice versa) and *always* in the most unexpected way.

Step 2 – Draw Up Your Storyline

This is, in very simple words, the plan of how your story is going to flow. When you begin to create your rough story-line, do not worry if it does not flow right away. You can gradually build it up.

In Appendix D, I've provided you with a storyline that's suitable for a creative writing work. Here, I would like to concentrate on how drawing up a proper storyline would assist in business.

Assume this: you have found out that a colleague of yours is about to be sacked. He has, no doubt, been performing badly at work. He has withdrawn from everyone and is all but a recluse. It would be to your advantage if he leaves the company as that opens up a spot for promotion for you. However, there's something bothering you and you decide to talk to him. After you listen to his side, you make up your mind to put your own neck on the line and speak out on his behalf. You risk everything, including losing your own job. You're planning to present your colleague's case to your bosses. How would you do this?

What do you think would be the outcome if you went up to your boss and said, "I want a word with you. How can you even think of letting my colleague go?" Your boss is likely to be furious at your audacity.

Now, imagine what your boss's reaction would be if you took a different approach. You start by saying, "I'd like to tell you a story. It is about a boy who had a fantastic ability to grasp and decipher information. He was like a store house of information…" Thereafter, you tell him that the boy grew up, got married and settled into family life in suburbia. He forgot his dream of managing a whole database of information and worked in sales. He was not very good at it but the job paid the bills. About a year ago, his wife was diagnosed with breast cancer. They told no one but visited every single doctor they could. They used up their savings and one day there was no more money left. He started to do work for others on the quiet and as a result they could pay the medical bills. Only that year at work he was not paid a bonus. His car was repossessed and soon, he had to move to a flat as they had mortgaged the house as well.

At the end of this story, told with massive amounts of emotion and drama, you ask your boss, "Do you know who I'm talking about?"

If you have not already guessed, this is a true story. I've changed some of the details but the fact remains that the man retained his job. Indeed, he was re-evaluated and moved to another department – the Knowledge Management Department. His spouse recovered from her illness and, I'm happy to say, they're expecting their first child. What of the storyteller? As luck would have it, he was promoted to the position his colleague had just vacated.

Step 3 – Adding Texture
There are three ways in which you can add texture to your tale.

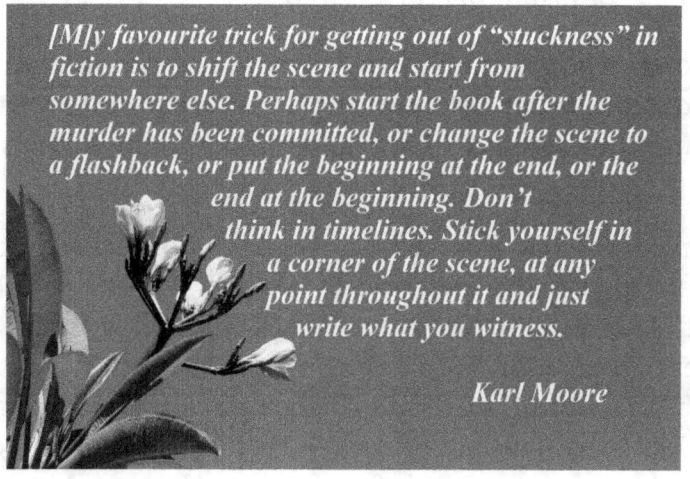

[M]y favourite trick for getting out of "stuckness" in fiction is to shift the scene and start from somewhere else. Perhaps start the book after the murder has been committed, or change the scene to a flashback, or put the beginning at the end, or the end at the beginning. Don't think in timelines. Stick yourself in a corner of the scene, at any point throughout it and just write what you witness.

Karl Moore

1. Flashback

It is not always necessary to add a flashback in any story you tell. Your story will still be great without a flashback. But add a flashback and you'll add that extra dramatic layer – you can show an event in the past that has direct relevance to what is happening in the present. It can reveal how a previous experience influences the way a person acts or thinks.

Two things to be cautious about: One, never have a flashback within a flashback. It just makes the entire story unnecessarily complicated. Two, always use the past perfect tense in flashbacks; simply put, this means using the word 'had' – she had gone to meet him; he had eaten his pie.

2. Foreshadowing

Have you ever wondered why, early on in a movie, the camera focuses on useless items like a flower or a pin or earring? This technique is called foreshadowing. It's used for planting, in the audience's mind, facts which at that time do not seem significant but which will be vital in a later part of a story.

In our story with the helpful colleague, the storyteller could say something like, "this company has been very good to him. The employers even paid for him to learn how to drive a car ..." and move on to the next topic. Much later, the storyteller could bring the focus back to how good the company have been when he says something like, "...nothing given to this employee has been wasted. For instance, he used the driving skills he learnt to drive his wife to and from the hospital to get treatment."

3. Sub-plots

These are secondary or subsidiary episodes that run alongside the main plot. They offer the chance for the minor characters to have their own dramas or for the hero to have to deal with a drama quite separate from the major conflict. A word of caution: a sub-plot should add to the story, but not compete with it. The themes can be reinforced in a sub-plot.

Concluding Comments

I've shown you the most widely used ways of putting together the vital plots for a gripping story. There are, of course, other ways you can do this, but classic strategies are tried and tested. What I suggest you do the next time you hear a story that grips you is spend a little time, "deconstructing" the tale. Find out what made it interesting. Look at how the storyteller has used all of the ingredients to make that tale exciting. For now, let's look at the final step of how to create your own story.

STEP 7 – IT'S ALL A MATTER OF STYLE

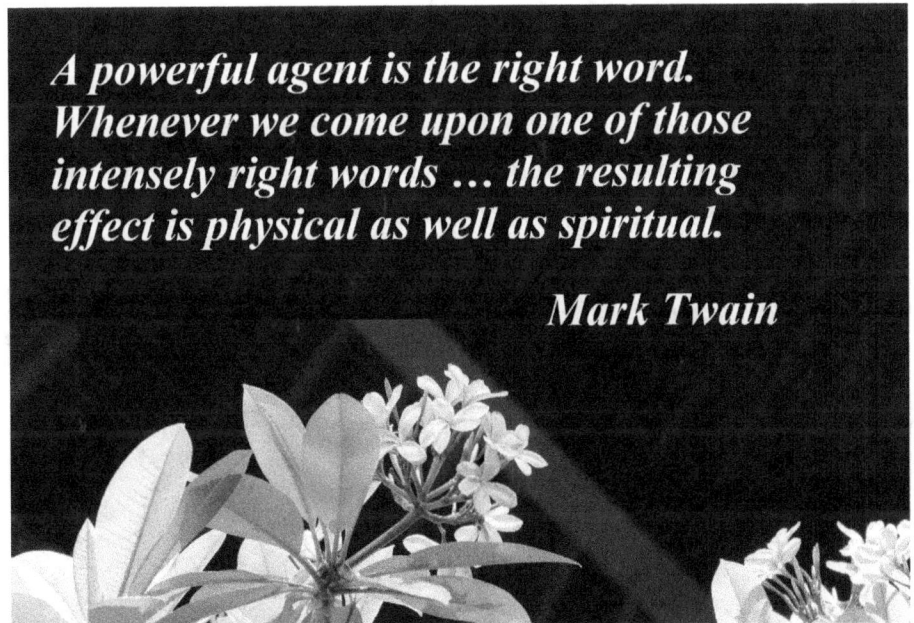

A powerful agent is the right word. Whenever we come upon one of those intensely right words ... the resulting effect is physical as well as spiritual.

Mark Twain

In 1946, in an essay called, *Politics and the English Language*, George Orwell discussed how language could be used and abused. He shared certain rules which, to this day, make perfect sense for anyone who wishes to communicate effectively in English. The essence of what George Orwell shares is that a scrupulous storyteller, in every sentence he utters, must ask himself the following questions:

1. What am I trying to say?

2. What words will express it best?
3. What image or idiom will make it clearer?
4. Could I put it more succinctly?
5. Have I said anything that is avoidably ugly?
6. Never use a metaphor, simile, or other figure of speech which you are used to seeing in print.
7. Never use a long word where a short one will do.
8. If it is possible to cut a word out, always cut it out.
9. Never use the passive where you can use the active.
10. Never use a foreign phrase or scientific jargon if you can think of an everyday English equivalent.
11. Break any of these rules sooner than say anything outright barbarous.

As you keep George Orwell's advice in mind, remember that each person has their own style of narrating a tale. The following are some of the techniques that can help you develop your own style of storytelling.

Dynamic Dialogue

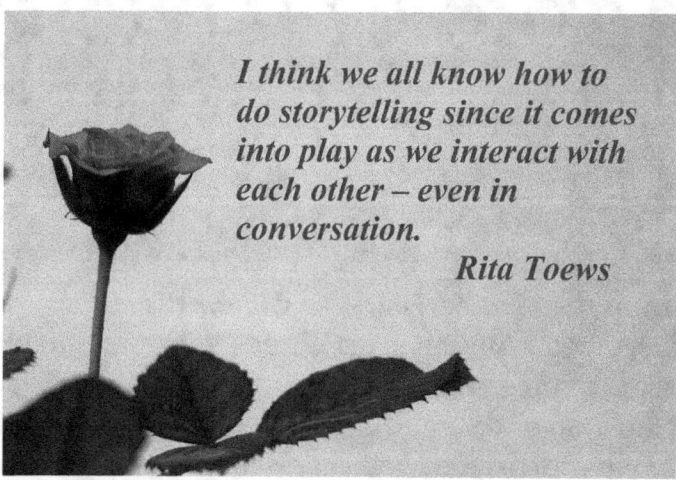

I think we all know how to do storytelling since it comes into play as we interact with each other – even in conversation.

Rita Toews

In very simple terms, the application of dynamic dialogue will depend on whether your narration is verbal as opposed to written. For example, in written form, a piece of dialogue might read as follows:

Are we going out tonight? I certainly am. Why don't you come along? But you'll need to supply the wheels. Pick me up at eight, OK?"

In spoken form, a piece of dialogue would probably read,

When are we going out tonight? Err .. um ... I hadn't really given it much thought. Hmmm... how about 7.30? Is that too early? Yes, I suppose it might be. How about nine – no, too late. I suppose it'll have to be about eight. Can you pick me, my car's playing up all over again.

Can you see the difference?

So, depending on your type of narration, you must make it believable to your audience.

Furthermore, the functions of your dialogue are not just for the purpose of chatting but it must provide vital information for your audience. The same principles apply to storytelling in a business context. The four functions of dialogue in a story are:

1. To progress the story.
2. To create excitement.
3. To tell the audience more about the character's background.
4. To give pace to a story.

Now, let's analyse each of these in a little more detail.

1. To progress the story
Your dialogue should always take your story to the next level. For example:

> "Mark is not here. I arrived early this morning and decided to surprise him. The house is such a mess, I tell you. I am busy cleaning the place. I am sorry but I cannot help you with this. I don't know where he left the keys to the garage," said Sue to Jane, the village busy-body.
>
> "Strange you should say this. I saw Mark only yesterday. He

said that as you were due back today, he was going to stay in and clean the place and surely he would be able to find the keys as he was cleaning up. I guess he went off with that lady after all," answered Jane.

"What lady?" asked Sue with a tinge of shock in her voice.

"Oh. Don't get me wrong. I don't think it's anything serious. When we were speaking in town yesterday, this lady came up to him and I heard him say that he would meet her at her place in an hour's time," Sue replied.

Can you see how the tone of the story changed as it progressed?

2. To create excitement
This is a wonderful way to create excitement in your narration.

"Oh my God, Mark. How could you do this to me?" exclaimed Sue as she opened the door to the bedroom in their guest house by the beach. On the bed she saw her husband, Mark, with Claudia.

3. To tell the audience more about the characters' and the narrator's background.
When you narrate your own story, unconsciously you are telling your audience how old you are, where you come from, how well educated you are and how confident you are.

The dialogue you write gives your characters' backgrounds too. The best example I can give you is Professor Henry Higgins and Eliza from George Bernard Shaw's *Pygmalion*, or as Hollywood entitled it, *My Fair Lady*. Professor Higgins spoke in "received pronunciation" or "The Queen's English" which denoted him as an upper class Englishman of the period. He taught Eliza how to speak as he did instead of as a cockney, and that alone transformed her from a flower girl into a lady.

4. To give pace to a story
Instead of spending hours describing the terrible conditions of

a particular place, you can always economise by using dialogue. For example, you can say, "Paul summed it up best. 'What a dump! Really, the place was smelly."

Grammar

I am not going to teach you grammar here but there are certain things I would like to point out.

Split infinitives:
Observe this sentence:
I used to continually talk about my writing

The words "to talk", which together are the infinitive form of the verb, have been split by the word "continually". It would have been better to say *I used to talk continually about my writing.*

You should also write in full sentences. For example, when you are giving a speech, although grammatically "I think" is correct but when you speak it out loud, it does not make sense.

Be very clear about what you are saying at all times. For example, if I say, "I had to spend several weeks away from my home in Australia which I did not like." Which of the two statements below do I mean?

- I had to spend several weeks away from my home. I spent that time in Australia and I did not like it.
- My home is in Australia. I had to spend several weeks away from it and did not like it.

Here's another example: I once had a conversation with a gentleman that went something like this:

Mr. X: Let me tell you the story of Adam. His father, Steven was looking after him. He was really a very nice guy but was born with deformities. He grew up in an unhappy home and his father used to abuse him. He ended up going to jail you know.

I was confused. There were many thoughts going through my mind:

1. Was Adam a nice guy but born with deformities?
2. Was Steven a nice guy but born with deformities?
3. Did Adam grow up in an unhappy home where Steven used to abuse him?
4. Did Steven grow up in an unhappy home where Adam's grandfather abused Steven?
5. And really, who ended up going to jail - the grandfather, Steven or Adam?

Can you see how confusing this statement was? To be precise in what you say is really an art. It is not something you can get right immediately. However, the moment you begin to try, it will bear fruit. People will understand you better and your storytelling skills will improve dramatically.

Punctuation

Ensure you use punctuation to produce the cadence and "correct" meaning of your words and sentences.

Richard Johnson

When people speak to each other, they make their meaning clear by pausing between groups of words, by putting emphasis on certain words and by using gestures. When you write, you will need to show these very things by using punctuation. The easiest way to show you the importance of punctuation is by asking you to read the following paragraph.

we have to use punctuation which includes full stops commas hyphens and so on and forth to make each and every sentence we utter when telling our great story it helps to define the tale set the tone and give dynamic quality to the story otherwise reading a passage such as this will put any member of the audience to sleep

Now, re-read this very paragraph, re-written with proper punctuation.

We have to use punctuation, which includes full stops, commas, hy-

phens and so on and forth, to make each and every sentence we utter when telling our great story. It helps to define the tale, set the tone and give dynamic quality to the story. Otherwise reading a passage such as this will put any member of the audience to sleep.

You see, punctuation tells us where the pauses should be.

11 Rules of Punctuation

There are 11 punctuation marks I would like to look at, namely:
1. The Full Stop
2. The Comma
3. The Colon
4. The Semi-Colon
5. The Hyphen
6. Inverted Commas
7. Brackets
8. The Dash
9. The Apostrophe
10. Question Mark
11. The Exclamation Mark

Each of these has guidelines for their proper use. Once you've become a master storyteller, you will know how to bend the rules to get maximum effect, but you must be aware of the underlying rules.

Full Stop (.)

The full stop is the strongest mark which indicates the end of a sentence, or one coherent statement or thought. This is a longer than one that comes after a comma or semi-colon or colon. It can also be used after an abbreviation. When you start a new sentence after a full stop, you will always start with a capital letter. However, when a full stop follows an abbreviation, you do not use a capital letter. For example:

The months of the year, September, October, November etc. may be abbreviated to Sept., Oct., Nov.

The Comma (,)

The comma indicates a lesser pause than the full stop. Writers of yesteryear tended to write long sentences with many commas in them. The trend now is to use fewer commas and write shorter sentences. Here is an example of a text, punctuated by many commas. It is written by John Mortimer, the author of the Rumpole novels. In the story, *Rumpole and the Bubble Reputation*, he writes:

Crime is about life, death and the liberty of the subject; civil law is entirely concerned with that most tedious of all topics, money. Criminal law requires an expert knowledge of bloodstains, policemen's notebooks and the dark flow of human passion, as well as the argot currently in use around the Elephant and Castle. Civil law calls for a close study of such yawn-producing matters as bills of exchange, negotiable instruments and charter parties. It is true, of course, that the most enthralling murder produces only a small and long-delayed Legal Aid cheque, sufficient to buy a couple of dinners at some Sunday supplement eaterie for the learned friends who practise daily in the commercial courts.

Here are the main uses of commas.

- Commas marks off lists in a list: *I saw pens, rubbers, rules and paper on her desk.*

- You can use commas to separate two or more adjectives connected to a noun. This is similar to separating items in a list: *John Mortimer is a talented, prolific writer.*

- If you want to put a phrase into a sentence to make the sentence clearer or give greater explanation, you should surround that phrase with commas. Take the simple sentence:

Andrea arrived early at her office.
Say that you'd like to add this phrase – *Andrea is a very busy woman.*

With the use of commas, there is no need to repeat the word 'Andrea'. We do not need to say: *Andrea arrived early at her office. Andrea is a very busy woman.*

Use commas to say: *Andrea, who is a very busy woman, arrived early at her office.*

Important tip: If you can take the part surrounded by the commas out of the sentence and the sentence still makes complete sense, then you will know you have placed the commas in the correct place.

If you placed the commas in the following places, it would be wrong:
Andrea who is, a very busy woman arrived early, at her office.

This is because the sentence would read: *Andrea who is at her office.* As you can see, it makes no sense at all.

- You can surround adverbs or conjunctions with commas, the most common ones being, *however, therefore* and *of course*.

The faces of these models, however, are not beautiful.
We will, of course, return your sugar bowl immediately.

- Adding information – or to the end of a sentence.

Andrew typed the article, but had to do it again because he had made a mistake.
Andrew typed the article again, although it was unnecessary.

- Direct speech is always marked off with a comma. For example:

He said, "I get really excited when I've completed my story."

The Colon (:)
The colon indicates a slightly lesser pause than a full stop. It is used when introducing a list such as this:

(i) January
(ii) February
(iii) March

Did you notice how I used the colon after the word 'this'?

The other place to use a colon is within a sentence where you make a statement and then give further details.

> *She felt he had only left her two alternatives: to join him for dinner and ignore his rude remarks, or to make a fuss and walk out.*

The Semi-Colon (;)
The semi-colon is stronger than a comma, but less strong than a colon or full stop. It is used to link two closely connected sentences into one; or to separate items in a "complex" list. (I used the semi-colon in that last sentence for the first reason.)

(1) Here is another example of a semi-colon used to join two closely connected sentences:

> *The gym was empty; everyone had left.*

(2) Here is an example where a semi-colon is used to separate a list of items where some or all of the other items have their own internal punctuation:

> *In his office there was a cluttered desk covered in papers, files and books; a battered, red leather chair; a safe and an ancient, rusty kettle.*

The Hyphen (-)
Never confuse the hyphen with a dash. A dash lengthens the pause between words, while a hyphen shortens it. There are 6 ways to use the hyphen.

(1) To link two or more words together to form a compound word:

> *son-in-law, court-martial*

(2) You can form a compound adjective by using a hyphen:

first-rate, well-known, far-reaching

Important tip: Only use the compound adjective when the noun it is describing immediately follows it.

John Mortimer is a well-known author

If the noun comes first, there is no need for the hyphen:

All authors in this literary festival are well known.

(3) Another use of the hyphen is to link certain prefixes like anti, ex and pro to a noun. For example:

anti-war
ex-wife
pro-Malaysian

(4) The hyphen helps in pronunciation. For example: co-operation. If the hyphen does not exist, there is a tendency to state it as cooperation where the 'oo' is pronounced in the same way as the "oo" in coop.

(5) Helps to define the meaning of a word.

Three inch sticks.

It could mean three sticks where each one of them is one inch long or, one stick which is three inches long. When you say three-inch sticks it clearly means sticks which are three inches in length.

(6) Hyphens can alter the meaning of words. For example:

His re-marked exam papers show that there was an error in the marking system.
He remarked on the fact that there might be an error in the marking system.

Inverted Commas (" ")

Inverted commas are used to indicated direct speech or quotation. There are two schools of thought about using single and double inverted commas. One is that single inverted commas should be used throughout, and if there is a need to use quotations or direct speech within a quote or a speech, then these should be shown within double inverted commas. The other view is that double inverted commas are used as the default and single inverted commas are the secondary form to be used within them. Neither is "right" or "wrong"; the important thing is to remain consistent throughout your story.

Brackets ( )
Brackets are used .to separate a sub clause within a sentence more strongly than it would be separated from the main clause between commas,

At present, Patricia (unlike other teachers in the school) does her very best to teach English to all the students.

Important tip: Just as with commas, if you can take the part surrounded by the brackets out of the sentence and the sentence still makes complete sense, then you will know you have placed the brackets in the correct place.

The Dash (–)
The dash is longer than the hyphen. You can use the dash instead of commas or brackets for more informality and greater emphasis, when separating a phrase or statement within a sentence:

> Mr. Blogs has a secretary – a very competent person – to do his typing and general clerical work.

As in the use of brackets and commas, if you remove the dashes, you will still have complete sentence.

Apostrophe (')
The apostrophe has two uses.

1. To show where a letter has been missed out.
    it's (it is)
    don't (do not)
    can't (cannot)
    doesn't (does not)

2. To show ownership

> *My father's house* – this means that the house belongs to my father.

What is the difference between these two sentences?
> *The lawyer's office.*
> *The lawyers' office.*

In the former, there is only one lawyer and it is his office.
In the latter, there are two or more lawyers and it is their office.

If the word already ends with an 's' then you can leave out the extra 's' following the apostrophe. For instance:
> *Dennis' shoes.*

Important tip: Correct use of the apostrophe is considered very important by editors and publishers.

Question Mark (?)
The rule here is very simple. You always use the question mark at the end of a direct question:
> *What time is it now?*
> *Where are you going tonight?*

You do not use question mark at the end of an indirect question:
> *Tell me where you are going tonight.*
> *Ask the watchman when he thinks the thief entered the house.*

The Exclamation Mark (!)
Use an exclamation mark at the end of a sentence to add emphasis and draw attention.
> *You must be joking!*
> *If you don't like the clothes you're wearing then, for God's sake, buy something you do like!*
> *Go away!*

Use exclamation marks sparingly for the simple reason that the overuse of it will detract from any impact you might wish to convey.

Things to avoid

Slang

I am aware that Bill Cosby will probably not be the best person to use to illustrate a point considering the furore around his court cases. However, he made an important point early in 2004 and I cannot find any other person who made the same point in the same or better way. Please, therefore, do not be angry with me for using what he said to illustrate my point. With that disclaimer made, let me share with you the comment he made in a speech he presented.

> "Ladies and gentlemen, the lower economic people are not holding up their end in this deal. These people are not parenting. They are buying things for kids – $500 sneakers for what? And won't spend $200 for *Hooked on Phonics*. They're standing on the corner and they can't speak English. I can't even talk the way these people talk: 'Why you ain't,' 'Where you is'... And I blamed the kid until I heard the mother talk. And then I heard the father talk... Everybody knows it's important to speak English except these knuckleheads... You can't be a doctor with that kind of crap coming out of your mouth!"

Cosby also targeted imprisoned blacks.

> "These are not political criminals," he said. "These are people going around stealing Coca-Cola. People getting shot in the back of the head over a piece of pound cake and then we run out and we are outraged, [saying] 'The cops shouldn't have shot him.' What the hell was he doing with the pound cake in his hand?"

The reason I raised this is because many people living in Asia may not know what a pound cake is. Indeed, it is only from access to American programmes on TV that you might know what a "knucklehead" is.

The lesson to learn from this is that when you use slang, you must ensure that your audience is aware of what it means.

If you suspect that they do not know what the words mean, you must take a moment and explain what it means. Otherwise, you will lose your audience... very fast!

Slang words should generally be avoided. It is said that it is used in everyday speech because people have poor vocabulary or lazy thinking. It is acceptable when Mr. Cosby uses examples like "Where you is", to make a point about slang; however, when he used the word "knucklehead" on his own behalf it immediately narrowed his audience. Only people exposed to American TV and life in the West would have understood this word.

Another danger of using too much slang in your storytelling is that these words come in and out of fashion very quickly, so your work may rapidly become dated. On the other hand, knowing the slang of a particular place or time can add authenticity to the period or setting of your story. I would, in any case, advise you to use your discretion as to how much slang you use.

Swearing
My advice is that you should never use swear words when narrating a tale. The operative word here is intentionally, because however much you try not to offend others, there's only so much you can do – what one person may consider as swearing may not be so to another. Here's an example of how this can happen. An author once referred to one of the characters in a biography he wrote as "a woman". When the book was published, there were many people who were offended that the word "woman" was used as they were of the opinion that it suggested someone of lower social status. When I asked what word the author should have used, the author was told that he should have used the word "lady". The problem is that whilst "woman" is defined as the "feminine word for man", "lady" is defined as "mistress".

Try to avoid clichés.
How many times have you read or heard, "His eyes were as wide

as silver dollars"? In the first place this phrase is overused, and in the second place, silver dollars these days are only slightly larger than quarters. In addition, people from the outside of the United States don't even know what a silver dollar looks like. Be original when using metaphors – though sometimes the most effective are the simplest:

> "Virtue is like a rich stone, best plain set" Francis Bacon *Of Beauty*.

He said, She said.
Many editors do not approve of stories that have "he said" and "she said" leading into dialogue. Use a variety of words – "she muttered/yelled/smiled..." – or lead in with some action by the speaker instead: "John adjusted his seat belt and turned to his wife. 'So, Jane, where do you want to have dinner?'"

Concluding Comments for It's All A Matter of Style

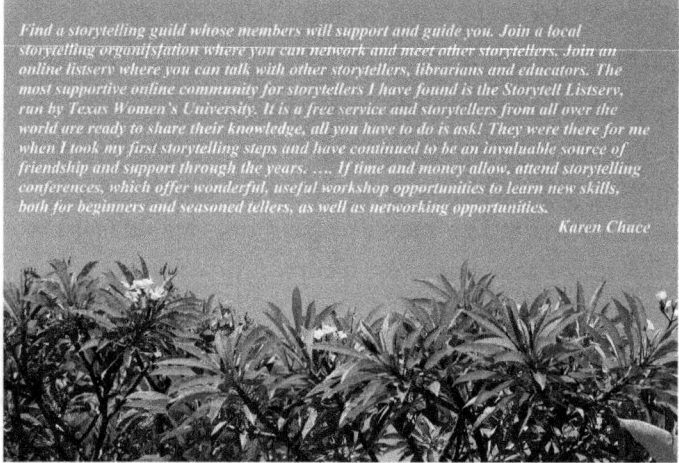

Find a storytelling guild whose members will support and guide you. Join a local storytelling organistation where you can network and meet other storytellers. Join an online listserv where you can talk with other storytellers, librarians and educators. The most supportive online community for storytellers I have found is the Storytell Listserv, run by Texas Women's University. It is a free service and storytellers from all over the world are ready to share their knowledge, all you have to do is ask! They were there for me when I took my first storytelling steps and have continued to be an invaluable source of friendship and support through the years. …. If time and money allow, attend storytelling conferences, which offer wonderful, useful workshop opportunities to learn new skills, both for beginners and seasoned tellers, as well as networking opportunities.
— Karen Chace

Style, like most other things, is subject to changing tastes. As you develop your own style, why not keep the words of Chandrika in mind:

> I believe that a story needs to have a judicious mixture of Setting, Plot, Theme, Character, Climax and Denouement...

A story may just capture a moment in time, freeze a point in space, or expose just one aspect of a character, but unless situation and character and theme blend, it will not grip. One cannot just put in the ingredients and hope to have a tasty dish. Judicious blending is of the utmost importance. [Then, p]lace a particular character in a situation and he will be propelled by his nature to behave in a certain manner. Create a particular situation and it will be pushed towards a conclusion, by its very circumstances... The third factor I always stress is style, the ability to write evocatively. Language is a jealous mistress. It is also a cruel taskmaster... For "how" a story is told is as important as "what" a story is about. To be able to do this, there is only one key – read, read read. Especially poetry. Unless you learn to make love to language, seduce phrases and words, be a painter, musician and carpenter, words will not resonate within.

CONCLUSION

> *Make your own opportunities. Go out there and do it... Don't be afraid to build your own opportunities. If you don't believe in your work, if you are not willing to be vulnerable in sharing it, then you cannot expect anyone else to respond to you. And on that note, community is so important – the solidarity offered in finding the right group of writers with whom to have discussions, organise events and writing sessions, get critiques from, just shoot off an email to when you've got a great passage or poem down, is powerful.*
>
> *Sharanya Manivannan*

In this book, I have shown you how to prepare yourself, both mentally and physically, for the challenge of telling a great story. Thereafter, I have shown you seven of the most important aspects of telling a great story. With the information listed in the appendices, you should have a broad overview of how to go about telling your great story.

It is worth saying that storytelling is a skill and like most, to become better at it, you need to practice. As you practice this art, you will develop your individual style and if you can introduce all of the ingredients we have looked at, there is no reason why you will not develop your story into great tale. As Lee Masterson puts it, "No matter how hard it gets or how many people tell you it can't be done – persist. Never give up on your dreams and goals.

Never allow anyone to denigrate those ideals. Never tell yourself you can't do it. Be positive. Believe in yourself and your vision of where you want your career to go, and then keep on persisting."

I hope that the comments by storytellers featured in this book have given you hope and encouragement. Still, as Leanne Johnson advises, "...you must seek out other storytellers... Find a guild, or story circle, or some place where you can try out your work in front of a supportive audience... Every month I meet with three other storytellers. We spend an entire day honestly critiquing our work. We started back in 1995, and it has become an invaluable process. Sometimes it is painful – when they say, 'Leanne, we don't get it, it's just not working.' But then four of us work together to polish the weak spots. We all benefit, and so do our audiences."

I will end this book with the words of Aldous Huxley: 'Words form the thread on which we string our experiences.' You see, once the thread is strong, the stories you weave from this single thread will create a stunning fabric; a story that will remain in the hearts and minds of the many people you tell it to.

I wish you all the success in this adventure that you have embarked upon. Happy storytelling!

APPENDIX A – PLANNING AND ANALYSING YOUR RESEARCH MATERIAL

Date of Research	
Title of Resource	
Medium of Resource – ☐ electronic publication ☐ library book ☐ reference book ☐ article in newspaper ☐ article in magazine ☐ other:	
Source of information: • Website URL • Full reference for the written piece	
Author and Contact Details	
Number of Words	

APPENDIX A – PLANNING AND ANALYSING YOUR RESEA...

Excerpts	
1. Why did you read this story? 2. Did you want to know how to perform a specific task? 3. Was the subject matter of this story interesting/fascinating? 4. Was it informative? 5. Was it written in an entertaining manner? Can you give an exact example of what made it so? 6. Was there a logical order to how the story was set out? 7. How did the story end? 8. Did you enjoy reading this story? 9. Would you read more work by this author?	
Copyright Issues	

APPENDIX B – INFORMATION FOR MARKET RESEARCH

Who is the target audience?	
What types of settings are suitable?	
What is the age range and gender of the people who generally read this magazine?	
Are the storylines in the magazines similar in all their stories?	
Is there any subject that is taboo – for instance, violence in any form, or style is unacceptable.	
How do you submit material to them? i.e., do they accept submissions via email or do you have to send your submission by post?	

APPENDIX C: CHARACTER PROFILE

Name	
Date of Birth	
Place of Birth	
Age at the time the story is told	
Gender	
Distinguishing features – how old does the character appear and does his/her appearance reflect his/her actual age?	
Background, social class and significant events in this person's life.	
Main character trait	

Appearance
   Hair
   Eyes
   Complexion
   Height/Build
   Skin colour and type
   Is s/he healthy? If not, why?	

Favourites: Character's favourite colour Character's favourite music	

Character's favourite food Character's favourite literature Character's favourite expressions Character's favourite form of transport How does this character spend a rainy day?	
Good habits	
Bad habits	
What does s/he like to do in his spare time?	
What does s/he dislike most in life?	
Relationships with his/her family	
Relationships with her/his friends	
Where has he lived?	
Does s/he like pets? If so, what kind?	

Strengths and what are his/her goals (both long term and short term)	
Weaknesses	
Problems	

APPENDIX D – SAMPLE STORYLINE

Jack is a schizophrenic patient who has been in and out of hospitals for the past five years. In the last few months, he has been having visions of a masked man who stalks women and then kills them. One day, in the hospital, he sees the back of the retreating form and is convinced that this is the person he sees in his visions. When he tries to tell his counsellor, she tells him that he is hallucinating and gives him more drugs. He tries to tell his wife but she does not believe him either.

At the police station, a police officer, Mandy, listens to her boss at a press conference telling the public about the recent spate of murders. Mandy tries to tell her boss that when she was still in the Police Academy, she remembers studying a case that fits this profile. He does not believe her and says that Mandy cannot be right as it's been a long time since she was in the Police Academy.

Meanwhile, Jack goes home to recuperate, but then he reads about a third murder. At that moment, he has another vision—one where he is being stalked. He realises that he'll be the next victim and panics. He goes to the police station to tell them what he knows. Unfortunately, no one believes him and he loses his temper. He is sedated and re-admitted into hospital. All this while, Mandy has been watching him from afar.

As time goes by Jack becomes frustrated. He keeps having the same visions, but he cannot see the face of the killer, just a clear birthmark somewhere on the inside of the arm.

Mandy is given menial tasks and becomes frustrated as well. But as she goes through some of her work, she comes across a story that suddenly makes her wonder whether this mad man's ravings are really true. For the next few months she tries many times to visit Jack but is constantly prevented by the doctor in charge.

One day, months later, Jack is being treated by the doctor when he suddenly begins to have visions. He sees the murderer approaching him whilst he is in the doctor's consulting room. All he sees is the birthmark. At that moment, he realises the doctor is washing her hands and Jack can see the birthmark on the inside of her arm. He is horrified to have finally identified the killer. The doctor turns around and when she realises Jack knows her secret, she confesses everything to him and tries to kill Jack. He defends himself by using one of the doctor's instruments and kills her. Mandy, who has gone against the orders of her bosses and continued to investigate this matter, has figured it all out. She arrives in the hospital in time to see Jack being led away by the police.

Months later, Mandy has resigned from her job. As she drives away, she hears the report on the radio that Jack has been convicted of manslaughter and sentenced to begin his prison term in a secure mental facility.

APPENDIX E – COPYRIGHT ISSUES FOR STORYTELLERS

My aim is to give you an overview of the issues that give rise to copyright and its infringement, what remedies can be sought by the injured party and what defences exist. To make it simpler, I'll consider only written work and not other material like photographs and so on.

As the UK and the USA are, without a doubt, the literary capitals of the world, I'll concentrate my efforts in explaining these issues in these two jurisdictions alone. Most of the time, they overlap but there are distinctions as well.

Please bear in mind that this is only a rough guide to the issue of copyright for storytellers. It is up to you to seek actual legal advice for any particular issue that you think you need to work on.

General Points

The premise from which to begin is this: Intellectual property protection comprises of patents, trademarks, industrial design, copyrights, geographical indications and layout designs of integrated circuits.

Copyright protects the particular form in which an author's idea has been expressed, not the idea itself. Generally speaking, plots or artistic ideas are not protected by copyright, but what is protected is the manner in which these ideas are presented.

In the UK, there is no need to publish a work for it to be considered protected. Hence, even manuscripts are protected by law.

The work must be original and by this, it is generally understood that it must be the "expressions of the thought" rather than just the thought itself that acquires copyright protection.

Infringement of works is what is commonly thought of as plagiarism. Remember that it is not that you have to copy word for word from a piece of work but that you have "substantially" copied a lot of it. This is a qualitative and not quantitative test. There are many cases dealing with this point and this report is not the place to go into the detail of case law. Nevertheless, based on the articles listed below, here is a brief explanation of the main points raised by most storytellers.

1. The UCLA Online Institute for Cyberspace Law and Policy. *Basic Principles of U.S. Copyright Law*. 10 February 2001 <**http://www.gseis.ucla.edu/iclp/cbasics.htm**.
2. Article 2: National Information Infrastructure. *Copyright Infringement.* **http://www.ladas.com/NII/CopyrightInfringement.html**

Definitions

The statute that governs copyright is the <u>Copyright, Designs & Patents Act 1988.</u> Under the Act, definitions are provided for several works:

Literary Work is defined as: "any work, other than a dramatic or musical work, which is written, spoken or sung", and accordingly includes:
1. a table or compilation other than a database,
2. a computer program,
3. preparatory design material for a computer program and
4. a database.

A musical work means: "a work consisting of music, exclusive of any words or action intended to be sung, spoken or performed with the music".

An artistic work means:
1. a graphic work, photograph, sculpture or collage, irrespective of artistic quality
2. a work of architecture being a building or model for a building, or
3. a work of artistic craftsmanship.'

These categories are not mutually exclusive – for example a film may be protected both as a film and as a dramatic work.

In the US, the governing statute is <u>The Copyright Statute.</u>

Questions

Question: When does copyright expire?
Answer: In the European Union, copyright in a written work lasts for the lifetime of the author and for a further 70 years from the end of the year of death.
In the US, for works created after 1 January 1978, the position is the same.
If the work is published posthumously, then copyright exists from the end of the year of publication.

Question: Do I need to seek copyright if I want to include an extract from a book, poem or article in my work?
Answer: If it's more than 70 years since the death of the author, or 70 years after publication of his/her work posthumously, generally the answer is "No."

Question: How much can I quote without infringing copyright?
Answer: Under the Copyright, Designs and Patents Act of 1988, you are restricted to up to 400 words of prose in a single extract of copyright work or a series of up to 300 words each, totalling no more than 800 words.

Question: What about poetry?
Answer: You are restricted to up to 40 lines of poetry, which must be no more than 25% of the poem.

Question: A newspaper has paid for a story. I now want to sell the story to a magazine. Can I do this?
Answer: Yes, provided you have not granted copyright or exclusive use to the newspaper. To do this, when you sell your story, make it clear that you are selling only First or Second Serial Rights, not your copyright.

Question: I had an idea for a story and I sent it to a magazine editor. I was not commissioned, but the editor used the ideas anyway. Can I sue the magazine?
Answer: There is no copyright in ideas, so you cannot sue a writer or a journal for using ideas that you've put forward. It is likely that you will find it very difficult to prove that the idea belonged to you and to you alone.

Question: I have found that someone has breached my copyright. What can I do?
Answer: The remedies are almost the same in both jurisdictions but you will have to consult a lawyer to figure out the finer details. Generally, the remedies available are:
a) Injunctions to restrain or prevent the infringement of copyrights.
b) Impounding or disposition of all the materials considered to be in breach of copyright.
c) Damages and profits – the copyright owner can ask for actual damages or profits suffered.

Question: I have been accused of breaching copyright. What defences are available to me?
Answer: There are many exceptions in both jurisdictions and you will need to consult a lawyer to determine

the exact defence available to you. However, some of the more common ones are:

a) Fair dealing for the purposes of non-commercial research or private study
b) Fair dealing for the purposes of criticism or review or reporting current events.
c) Incidental inclusion
d) Educational exceptions
e) Exceptions made for libraries and public administration
f) Where author cannot be identified
g) Making transient copies as part of technological process and backing it all up.
h) Public recitation where full acknowledgement has been given.

BIBLIOGRAPHY

Articles/Papers/Speeches

Orwell, George. *Politics and the English Language.* http://www.mtholyoke.edu/acad/intrel/orwell46.htm

Bill Cosby's remarks at a D.C. gala commemorating the 50th anniversary of the Brown v. Board of Education decision at the NAACP (2004). http://www.nydailynews.com/front/story/195095p-168538c.html

Books

Huxley, Aldous. *Brave New World.* Harper Perennial Modern Classics (October 17, 2006)

Backes, Laura. *Best Books for Kids Who (Think They) Hate to Read: 125 Books That Will Turn Any Child into a Lifelong Reader.* Three Rivers Press (July 17, 2001)

The Concise Oxford Dictionary of Current English: Thumb Index [Hardcover]. Ed. Della Thompson. Oxford University Press, USA; 9 edition (August 3, 1995)

WritersandArtists.co.uk. *Writers' and Artists' Yearbook.* A&C Black (June 30, 2010)

Merriam-Webster's Collegiate Dictionary. Merriam-Webster; 11th edition (July 2003)

The Oxford Dictionary of Quotations. Oxford University Press, USA; 7 edition (November 23, 2009)

Sir Ernest Gowers. *The Complete Plain Words.* David R Godine (November 1, 2002)

Partridge, Eric. *Usage and Abusage: A Guide to Good English.* W. W. Norton & Company; Revised edition edition (December 17, 1997)

C. Rajagopalachari. *The Mahabharat.* Bharatiya Vidya Bhavan/Mumbai/India; 52nd edition (January 1, 2005)

Mortimer, John. *Rumpole and the Age of Miracles.* Penguin (Non-Classics); Mti edition (December 1, 1989)

Movies
Junior. Dir. Ivan Reitman. Perfs. Arnold Schwarzenegger, Danny DeVito, Emma Thompson. Anamorphic, Closed-captioned, Color, DVD, Widescreen, NTSC. Universal Studios.

Casablanca. Humphrey Bogart (Actor), Ingrid Bergman (Actor) Black & White, DVD, Full Screen, NTSC (2010). Warner Home Video.

Wag The Dog. Dir. Barry Levinson. Dustin Hoffman (Actor), Robert De Niro (Actor), Anne Heche (Actor), Denis Leary (Actor), Willie Nelson (Actor). Closed-captioned, Color, Dolby, NTSC. Warner Home Video.

My Fair Lady. Dir. George Cukor. Audrey Hepburn (Actor), Rex Harrison (Actor). Color, DVD, Original recording remastered, Widescreen, NTSC. Paramount.

WHAT OTHERS ARE SAYING ABOUT 'HOW TO TELL A GREAT STORY'

"Whether writing nonfiction or delivering a speech, stories make your point memorable. Audiences love stories.'

Dan Poynter
http://ParaPublishing.com

"The most detailed, logical and literary analysis of how to create a memorable story yet. I was fascinated."

Joe Vitale
www.mrfire.com

"I bought your e-book and have read it. It is a great read and it has given me hope that I can also (with sufficient practice) become a good raconteur."

Lloyd Kaseke

"Since being introduced to *How to Tell a Great Story* and becoming a *Great StoryTelling Network* newsletter subscriber, I have laughed, been amazed, and always satisfied with the information provided. I highly recommend it to anyone who likes to improve their own story telling skills. While out on book signings, the most asked question is, 'How do I go about telling my story?' I always recommend *How to Tell a Great Story*."

Frank Landrey

www.CoachLandrey.com

"Wow, your book really taught me a lot about the art of storytelling. I found the information very helpful and can't wait to put your powerful tips into practice. If you're looking to improve your skills in this area then look no further!"

Michael Rasmussen
http://www.FreeAdvertisingForum.com

"... The ability to tell a story or anecdote – powerfully – is an absolutely vital tool to your success, no matter what you do. Stories are interesting, they touch the buyer in a way that can move them, and separate you from the competition. Aneeta's book can help greatly improve your abilities in this area; it will make you money and more effective in selling your ideas for the rest of your life."

Allan Boress
www.allanboress.com

ABOUT THE AUTHOR

The latest novel by Aneeta Sundararaj is a novel called *The Age of Smiling Secrets*. This book is the shortlisted (2 categories) for the Anugerah Buku 2020 (Book Awards 2020) organised by the National Library of Malaysia. As she reflects on this amazing achievement, she recounts how far she's come since she first started her writing career.

In 2003, Aneeta created, designed and developed the website, *How to Tell a Great Story* with the aim of sharing all she learnt about the craft of storytelling. Over the years, the website has grown and the various storytelling resources range from methods, ideas, research techniques, editing, storytelling in business and so on. In addition, she manages a free online newsletter (*Great Storytelling Network*) which continues to attract many columnists from all over the world.

Aneeta's writing has appeared in many magazines, ezines and journals. By contributing more than 250 feature articles to the national newspaper in Malaysia, *New Straits Times*, she has been fortunate enough to come into contact with people who have fascinating stories to tell. She strives to share some of them through her writing. Some of the other works by Aneeta include:

- *The Banana Leaf Men*
- *Ladoo Dog: Tales of a Sweet Dachshund*
- *Knowledge of Life: Tales of an Ayurveda Practitioner in Malaysia*
- *We Mark Your Memory: Writings from the Descendants of Indenture*
- *The Age of Smiling Secrets*
- *Two Snakes Whistling at the Same Time*

In addition, Aneeta welcomes contributions from her readers and, so far, many have submitted hundreds of articles about storytelling and reviews on various books and movies.

One special feature of the website is the column called *Blow Your Own Trumpet!* In this column, Aneeta has, over the years, interviewed hundreds of storytellers. You'd be surprised as to who these people are - they range from sociologists, tax consultants, motivational coaches, diplomats, authors and many more.

If you would like further information or feel you'll benefit from being interviewed by Aneeta, do not hesitate to contact her by sending an email to: editor@howtotellagreatstory.com

ABOUT HOW TO TELL A GREAT STORY

How To Tell A Great Story will equip you with powerful storytelling techniques that master storytellers have used throughout time to amaze and engage their audiences.

This simple, but powerful beginner's guidebook, makes learning storytelling techniques easy and explains things in simple language. When you read this book, you will learn how to…

- Start telling your own story quickly and effortlessly
- Construct a fascinating, well-structured story from scratch
- Use powerful master storytelling techniques to amaze your family and friends
- Find interesting ideas and inspiration for your stories
- Vividly and expertly describe the characters and settings in your stories.

www.ingramcontent.com/pod-product-compliance
Lightning Source LLC
Chambersburg PA
CBHW060852220526
45466CB00003B/1340